Cistercian Fathers Series.

Mary
Most Holy

Meditating With the Early Cistercians

Cistercian Fathers Series: Number Sixty-Five

Mary Most Holy

Meditating With the Early Cistercians

cistercian publications
Kalamazoo, Michigan

Texts Chosen and Edited by E. Rozanne Elder
Translations have previously appeared, or shall appear,
in volumes of the Cistercian Fathers Series
published by Cistercian Publications.

*The work of Cistercian Publications
is made possible in part by support from Western Michigan University
to the Institute of Cistercian Studies.*

cistercian publications
WMU Station
1903 West Michigan Avenue
Kalamazoo, MI 49008-5415

It has been decided
that all our monasteries
are to be founded
in honor of the queen of heaven and earth.

Cistercian Beginnings [1]

1. *Exordium cistercii 9.2.* This early account of the founding
of the 'New Monastery' at Cîteaux has been tentatively
dated to 1133-1150. See Chrysogonus Waddell, *Narrative and
Legislative Texts from Early Cîteaux* (Cîteaux-Commentarii
Cistercienses, 1999) 139-161, esp. 161.

Table of Contents

Abbreviations

CC	Corpus Christianorum series. Turnhout, Belgium: Brepols.
CCCM	Corpus Christianorum, Continuatio Medievalis. Turnhout: Brepols.
CCSL	Corpus Christianorum, Series Latina. Turnhout: Brepols.
CF	Cistercian Fathers series. Spencer-Kalamazoo: Cistercian Publications.
CS	Cistercian Studies series: Spencer-Kalamazoo: Cistercian Publications.
Ep.	Epistola [Letter]
PG	J.-P. Migne, Patrologia cursus completus, series Graeca
PL	J.-P. Migne, Patrologia cursus completus, series Latina
SBOp	*Sancti Bernardi Opera*, edd. Jean Leclercq, H. M. Rochais, C. H. Talbot. Rome: Editiones Cistercienses.

⁊ indicates that a word or several words in the text have been omitted

The Foundations of
Cistercian Devotion to Mary

The young Jewish girl who accepted an angel's invitation to become the mother of God Incarnate has down the centuries been admired as the quintessential example of christian life, acclaimed for her willing consent to God's will, and appealed to for her aid. Among the myriad Christians who have pondered her role in salvation history have been monks and nuns of the Cistercian Order. Each day in a cistercian monastery closes with the chanting of the haunting final antiphon, *Salve Regina*, and each of the seven daily offices includes a commemoration of Mary's unique vocation.

In singing Mary's praises, the 'White Monks' of Cîteaux, arriving—from our perspective—at about the mid-point of christian history, blended their voices with an already ancient choir. As the first Cistercians were building their monastery in the forests of Burgundy, crusader knights, and the pilgrims who followed along after them, were re-establishing contacts with the christian east and visiting the places Christ had walked. Perhaps in part because of their absence, european society was becoming a little less bellicose than it had been for centuries. Devotion to the gentle Mother of the Lord flowered at the same time, and the men who left all things to follow Christ at Cîteaux arrived in 'the wilderness' already devoted to *Domina nostra*, Our Lady. Once in the monastery they drew on a rich patristic and medieval store of treatises, homilies, and hymns which both formed and gave expression to their affectionate allegiance.

The Cistercians, quite literally, sought reform. Their goal was the re-formation of the human person to the likeness of God in which we were created. To this end, they aimed to reform monasticism by returning to a strict observance of Rule of Saint Benedict, pruning away pious and well-meant, but diverse and distracting, accretions that had built up over the early medieval centuries. The same quest for simplicity characterized their approach to theology; they returned to the sources—to Scripture and the writings of the Fathers of the Church. It was from this soil, enriched by contemporary spirituality, that their devotion to the Virgin flourished.

The Scriptural Cornerstone

Like the ancient bishops, monks, and theologians on whose work they built, the Cistercians read Scripture not simply as an historical document, but as the Word of God containing layers of meaning not apparent to the casual or unbelieving reader.[1] At the historical level they traced the record of God's activity from the instant of creation through the long history of the covenant people until the apostolic age. By an allegorical reading, they perceived within the events of this history prefigurations of the saving activity of Christ. At the tropological—sometimes called moral—level they saw in biblical persons and above all in Christ, his mother, and his disciples, examples of steadfast faith and godly living. Finally, by an anagogical reading, they contemplated the mysteries of God's eternal Being and the joyous anticipation of being forever in the divine presence. It was by peeling away these layers of hidden meaning that medieval monks, like the Fathers, could make claims for the Virgin which may not on the literal level be substantiated in Holy Writ.

On the historical level, they saw Mary as a young woman who, after a momentary hesitation, consented to become the unwed mother of God incarnate; who pondered in her heart her Son's preternatural wisdom but did not always understand his actions; who stood at the foot of the cross and

---

1. See Cassian, *The Conferences* 4.18; Bede, *De Tabernaculo et vasis eius ac vestibus sacerdotum*, 1.

watched him die, and who, with his closest followers, experienced his outpouring of the Holy Spirit at Pentecost.

Allegorical interpretation linked Old Testament promise and New Testament fulfilment. Christ himself had opened the door to this way of reading the Old Testament when he compared his own being lifted up on the cross with Moses lifting up the serpent in the wilderness.[2] As early and medieval Christians pondered Holy Scripture allegorically, they perceived foreshadowings of Mary's fruitful virginity in Aaron's walking staff, which burst into bloom[3]—'without water', Saint Bernard added[4]—and in the bush which Moses saw, burning and yet unconsummed.[5] The mother of Christ the Redeemer may be regarded allegorically as the mother of all those redeemed in Christ. As she nurtured the young Jesus, so she succors all who turn to Christ and become living members of his body, the Church, of which she is herself the type.[6] As the mother of Christ, the King of heaven, she assumes the royal dignity of queen mother. What is more, as queen of heaven and the mother of Christians, she can be appealed to for comfort and support when life seems unfair, people thoughtless, and events disappointing.

By a tropological reading, Mary provides the quintessential example of christian response to God. Of her own free choice, she consented to God's invitation. She did not suppress, but voiced, her doubts, and then consciously and deliberately conformed her will to the divine will. In her care for the child Jesus, she gives all mothers—all parents—a model of nurturing love.

On the anagogical level, the relationship between Mary and her Son reveals something of the ineffable mystery of the utter, eternal love which holds all creation in being and in relationship with God, the source and stay of all that is.

---

2. Jn 3:14.
3. Num 17:8.
4. See below, page 43.
5. Ex 3:2.
6. See below, p. 344.

The Patristic Foundation

After the Bible itself, the most formative books for monastic *lectio divina*, sacred reading, were commentaries on Scripture and homilies by the Fathers of the Church, sometimes known through *florilegia*, anthologies of passages selected from their works. The Mother of Christ is mentioned in the works of these learned preachers and exegetes of the first five centuries chiefly as she figured in the development of christological doctrine. Prevailing patristic opinion at the dawn of the fifth century is summarized by Epiphanius of Salamis (†403). While twelfth-century Cistercians did not read his works, written in Greek, he reflects a broad consensus, and the aspects of her life which he highlighted long remained the subjects of discussion:[7] her virginity, her sinlessness, and the ending of her life.

Epiphanius asserted that Mary had remained perpetually a virgin,[8] and that 'she never did anything wrong as regards fleshly actions but remained stainless.'[9] With no evidence whatever about how her life ended, he raised three possibilities: if she died, she died in virginity and honor; if she was martyred, as many believed had been foretold by Simeon at Jesus' presentation in the Temple,[10] then 'she dwells among those who enjoy the repose of the blessed'; and if she continued to live, then 'no one knows exactly what her end was.'[11]

In 431, the third ecumenical council, meeting at Ephesus to attempt to settle the great christological questions which had long occupied the Church, opened the floodgates to reflec-

---

7. See Luigi Gambero, *Mary and the Fathers of the Church: The Blessed Virgin Mary in Patristic Thought*. First published Milan 1991, translated by Thomas Buffer (San Francisco: Ignatius Press, 1999) 120-130. Epiphanius, unlike most other exegetes, also identified Mary with the woman in the Apocalypse: *Adversus Haereses* 78.11; PG 42:716. Cf. Rev 12.
8. *Adversus Haereses* 78.6; PG 42:705D.
9. *Adversus Haereses* 42.12; PG 41:77B.
10. Lk 2:35: a sword will pierce through your own heart.
11. *Adversus Haereses* 78.23; PG 42:737.

tion on the Lord's mother by officially designating her *Theotokos*, bearer of God. Objections were raised by some who preferred a more literal *Christokos*, bearer of Christ, but they were swept away by those intent on affirming the absolute oneness of Christ's person. Mary the mother of the human Jesus is Mary the mother of God, for Jesus is God incarnate. *Theotokos*—expressed variously in Latin as *Mater Dei*, mother of God, *Dei Genetrix*, begetter of God, or *Deipara*, bearer of God—came into the christian vocabulary and into the hearts and minds of Christians east and west.

In the west, learned opinion did not differ greatly from that of the east, although popular devotion to Mary lagged far behind the affective attachment of people living in close proximity to the places where she had once dwelt.[12] As Saint Paul[13] had compared the first Adam, who introduced sin into the world, with Christ, the second Adam who vanquished sin and death, so western exegetes contrasted Mary, the virgin who obeyed, with Eve, the virgin who disobeyed.[14] Mary's trust in the angel was compared with Eve's confidence in the serpent, and Eve's offspring, who murdered his brother, with Mary's Son, who saved Israel, 'his brother in the flesh'.[15]

Mary's virginity at Christ's conception was affirmed by both Scripture and tradition.[16] There were those who doubted that she had remained perpetually a virgin,[17] but most Christians considered unacceptable the idea that Jesus' mother had 'known Joseph' after Christ's birth.[18] Ambrose of Milan († 397), a great supporter of the consecrated virginal life, praised her as 'virgin in mind as well as body'.[19] The woman whom he

---

12. On the earliest developments of marian devotion in the east, see Stephen Shoemaker, *Ancient Traditions of the Virgin Mary's Dormition and Assumption* (Oxford:University Press, 2002).

13. 1 Cor 15:45.

14. Irenaeus of Lyons († c. 202): *Adversus Haereses* 3.22; PG 7:959-960.

15. Tertullian († c. 200), *De carne Christi* 17.5; PL 2:828.

16. Lk 1:27, 34-35. Cf. Nicene-Constantinopolitan Creed.

17. Tertullian, *De monogamia* 8.2; PL 2:989.

18. E.g. Hilary of Poitiers († c. 367): *In Matthaeum 13*; PL 9:921.

19. *De virginibus* 2.7; PL 16:220.

did not hesitate to call 'Mother of God'[20] Ambrose held up as the model of the consecrated life and a type of the Church,[21] that is, a prototype of humankind redeemed in Christ. He dismissed the still persistent rumor that she had suffered martyrdom[22] and suggested that she was 'not altogether ignorant of the heavenly mysteries.'[23]

The colossus of latin theologians and the source of most early medieval theological opinion, Augustine of Hippo († 430), regarded an understanding of Mary integral to the discernment of Christ's full humanity and full divinity. In her he saw the prototype of obedience and virginity, and the anti-type of Eve. Like Ambrose, he pointed to the correlation between Mary and the Church, considering both of them mother in charity and virgin in integrity.[24] Unlike Ambrose, Augustine referred to her, not as Mother of God, but simply as *mater Domini*, 'the Lord's mother'. The bishop of Hippo was 'the first in the West to deduce from Mary's answer to Gabriel at the Annunciation that she had already taken a vow of virginity'[25] and he believed that she had perpetually remained a virgin before, during, and after childbirth.[26] As the wife of Joseph, who acted as her protector in her dedicated virginity,[27] and as the virgin mother, he considered her the perfect model for consecrated virgins[28] and for faithful matrons.[29]

20. *Hexaemeron* 5.20.65; *De virginibus* 2.2.7.

21. *Expositio in Lucam* 2.7; PL 15:1635-1636.

22. *Expositio evangelii secundum Lucam* 2.61; PL 15:1574.

23. *Ibid.*: Et ideo prudentiam Mariae haud ignarem mysterii coelestis ostendit. . . .

24. Sermon 22.10A. See below, note 29.

25. Mary Clayton, *The Cult of the Virgin Mary in Anglo-Saxon England* (Cambridge UP 1990) 12–citing H. Barré, *Prières anciennes de l'occident à la mère du Sauveur* (Paris 1963) 30.

26. *Sermo* 291.5-6: Virgo es, sancta es, votum vouisti. Cf. *Sermo* 196.1: Virgo concepit...virgo peperit...post partum, virgo permansit. Augustine specifically condemned Antidicomaritae who denied Mary's perpetual virginity; Jovinianistae, who denied her virginity *in partu*; and Helvidiani, who accepted Helvidius' opinion that Mary had other sons. (see below, n. 29.)

27. Clayton citing Barré, as above, n. 25.   28. *Sermo* 51.26; PL 38:348.

29. *Contra Faustum* 23.8; PL 42:470. For a thorough summary of Augustine's marian teaching, see Daniel E. Doyle, OSA, 'Mary, Mother of God', in Allan D. Fitzgerald OSA, *Augustine through the Ages* (Grand Rapids: Eerdmans, 1999) 545.

The Early Medieval Setback

With Augustine's death in 430 the west entered a lingering twilight of theological reflection. Cut off for all practical purposes from the Church in the east, western Christians became preoccupied with coping with wave after wave of invaders who pushed across the indefensible frontiers of the western Roman Empire. From the fifth century until the tenth, barbarians[30] pillaged, conquered, displaced, or absorbed Romans and romanized native peoples, battled with one another over land and loot, and carved up as their own property the territory which had constituted the once invincible Empire. No sooner did they settle down than, very often, new marauders arrived and the cycle repeated itself. Amidst the chaos, the bishops of the church provided the only effective, civilizing leadership. The only havens of learning and relative peace were monasteries. Neither was safe and neither bishops nor monks had the time or within a short while the tools for theological reflection.

Trying to teach their new charges the rudiments of the faith kept bishops busy. As they settled in, the barbarians adopted Christianity, but they converted more out of tribal loyalty than personal conviction. Their knowledge of doctrine long remained tenuous, their grasp of Scripture rudimentary, and their resistance to christian moral demands resilient. Yet before long, these newly christianized barbarians were claiming episcopal rank and privilege for themselves, without noticeably modifying their habits. The descendants of these converts, caught in the early medieval world of unremitting warfare and sudden violent death, focused their hopes for a better life on Christ the Judge and fixed their yearning for temporal succor on the help of local holy men and women buried—or presumed to be buried—nearby and therefore

---

30. The original meaning was 'bearded', a distinguishing feature in a society of clean-shaven men. The modern meaning tells all about how the Romans perceived the behaviour of these bearded warriors.

'closely tied to the places men knew.'[31] Carolingian monks
might urge calling on Mary's prayers 'because we cannot find
anyone more powerful in merits for placating the wrath of
the Judge'[32] but God's power was popularly believed to be
concentrated at the place where a saint's body rested.[33] The
absence of marian relics, while it fostered belief in her assumption into heaven, therefore meant that until the eleventh century only a very few churches and monasteries in
the West were dedicated to her or fostered her cult.[34] Only
in the late eighth and ninth centuries, when "'by the impu-
dence of certain brethren" questions were being raised for
the first time concerning the doctrine of Mary'[35] did a dis-
tinctively western understanding of her role began to emerge.
By then she was universally believed to have been sanctified
and cleansed of sin by the Holy Spirit and, having therefore
reversed Eve's curse,[36] to have borne Christ without the pain
and suffering which curses other postlapsarian women. That
she might sometimes appear to believers had already been
confirmed by Pope Saint Gregory the Great († 604), who,
incidentally, also provides evidence of the existence of icons
of the Virgin.[37] Her perpetual virginity was rarely doubted
by celibate monks who, like the early medieval writer
Paschasius Radbertus of Corbie († c. 865) found compelling
scriptural proof in an allegorical reading of Ezekiel 44:12: *this
gate shall remain shut, for the Lord, the God of Israel, has entered by it.*

31. R. W. Southern, *The Making of the Middle Ages* (New Haven: Yale, 1953) 242.
32. Ratramnus of Corbie, *Sermo* 208.11 (*De assumptione*); PL 39.2134: . . . quia
nec potiorem meritis invenimus ad placandam irae Judicis quam te . . .
33. See Peter Brown, *The Cult of the Saints: Its Rise and Function in Latin
Christianity* (Chicago: University of Chicago Press, 1981).
34. See Southern (above, n. 31), 252. Clayton (n.25), 61.
35. Jaroslav Pelikan, *The Growth of Medieval Theology (600-1300)*, volume 3 of
his *The Christian Tradition. A History of the Development of Doctrine* (Chicago:
University of Chicago Press, 1978) 69, citing Paschasius Radbertus, *De partu
Mariae* 1. Pelikan's detailed description of 'Mary as Mediatrix', pages 160-174,
has provided several of my examples, and is well worth consulting.
36. Genesis 3:16.
37. *Ep.* 9.52; PL 77:990-991.

The Liturgical Framework

How Christians worship forms what they believe and how they believe it. By the end of the seventh century four liturgical festivals associated with Mary had been introduced into the Latin Church from the east. Two of them—the Annunciation on 25 March and the Presentation in the Temple on 2 February—mark events in Christ's life at which his mother was present; the other two—Mary's Assumption on 15 August and her Nativity on 8 September—are explicitly marian feasts which parallel the dominical feasts of Ascension and Christmas. The annual celebration of these four feast days, the lessons read on them, and the hymns and antiphons composed for monastic Offices and Mass lodged themselves in people's memories and provided the foundation on which marian devotion and marian theology were to be built in the Middle Ages and inherited by the White Monks.

For the first two feasts the Gospel of Luke provides a scriptural foundation; the latter were underpinned, not by Scripture, but by apocryphal literature which had begun to circulate—again in the east—as early as the second century. The apocryphal accounts provided details of Mary's birth and parentage[38] and recounted her death and passage into paradise.[39] While they informed popular piety in the Middle Ages, these narratives were treated with a great deal of caution by the literate, who for the most part insisted that when neither Scripture nor the Fathers provide information on a subject, then reverent prudence requires silence. Most writers agreed, for example, that 'while we confess that she is exalted above

---

38. See the *Protoevangelium of James.* Translated by James K. Elliott, *The Apocryphal New Testament* (Oxford: Clarendon, 1993). Also translated by Oscar Cullman and A. J. B. Higgins, in Ron Cameron, ed., *The Other Gospels. Non-Canonical Gospel Texts* (Philadelphia: Westminster, 1982) 109-121.
39. On the various families of marian apocrypha, see Shoemaker (above, n. 12).

the choirs of angels in heaven... we dare not affirm that the resurrection of her body has already taken place, since we know that this has not been declared by the holy fathers.'[40]

Yet while some counselled not relying on apocryphal tales when 'no catholic history gives an account of the way she ascended to the heavenly realm,'[41] others expressed a greater certitude about events. The earliest apocryphal accounts of the *Theotokos'* death claimed that her body still rests under the tree of life in Paradise awaiting the general resurrection at the second coming.[42] Gregory, bishop of Tours, writing in the late sixth century, on the other hand, maintained on the testimony of one of the stories in circulation[43] that:

> ...when blessed Mary, having completed the course of her earthly life, was about to be called from this world, the apostles gathered from the ends of the earth at her home... And behold, the Lord Jesus came with his angels and, taking her soul, handed it over to the archangel Michael and withdrew. At dawn the apostles lifted up her body on a pallet, laid it in a tomb, and kept watch over it, awaiting the coming of the Lord. And lo, the Lord appeared again to them and ordered that

40. Atto of Vercelli (mid tenth century), *Sermo* 17; PL 134: 856-7 Corporis vero ejus jam factam resurrectionem affirmare minime audemus, quia nec a sanctis Patribus hoc declaratum esse cognoscimus... Tamen sive in corpore, sive extra corpus, super choros angelorum in coelis exaltam confitemur.... [reversed in the translation].

41. Ambrose Autpert (†784), *Sermo* 208.3; PL 39:2130: Sed quo ordine hinc ad superna transierit regna, nulla catholica narrat historia, Non solum autem respuere apocrypha, uerum etiam ignorare dicitur haud eadem Dei Ecclesia. Et quidem sunt nonnulla sine autoris nomine de eius assumptione conscriptra; quae, ut dixi, ita cauentur...

42. For examples, see Shoemaker (above, n. 12), and Brian E. Daley SJ, trans., *On the Dormition of Mary: Early Patristic Homilies* (Crestwood, NY: St Vladimir's Seminary Press, 1998).

43. Gambero (note 7), 353, asserts that Gregory was using a translation of apocryphal narratives which no longer exists.

her holy body be taken and carried up into
paradise. There it now is, joined once more
to her soul, exulting with the elect, rejoicing
in the eternal blessings that will have no
end.[44]

A century later, Archbishop Isidore of Seville († 636) had
enough confidence in his source material to pinpoint the
location of her now empty tomb in the Valley of Jehoshaphat,[45]
as half a century later did an Irish monk-pilgrim, who admitted, 'But how or when or by what persons her holy remains
were removed from this sepulchre, and in what place she
awaits the resurrection, no one, they say, can know for sure'.[46]

44. *Glory of the Martyrs = Liber miraculorum*, 1: *De gloria beatorum martyrum* 4; PL
71:708. Denique impleto a beata Maria hujus vitae cursu, cum jam vocaretur
a saeculo, congregati sunt omnes apostoli de singulis regionibus ad domum
ejus. Cumque audiissent quia esset assumenda de mundo, vigilabant cum
ea simul: et ecce Dominus Jesus advenit cum angelis suis, et accipiens
animam ejus, tradidit Michaeli archangelo, et recessit. Diluculo autem
levaverunt apostoli cum lectulo corpus ejus, posueruntque illud in
monumento, et custodiebant ipsum, adventum Domini praestolantes. Et
ecce iterum adstitit eis Dominus, susceptumque corpus sanctum in nube
deferri jussit in paradisum: ubi nunc, resumpta anima, cum electis ejus
exsultans, aeternitatis bonis, nullo occasuris fine, perfruitur.
45. Isidore, *Quaestiones in Genesim* 2.18; PL 83:148-149: Specialiter tamen nulla
docet historia, Mariam gladii animaduersione peremptam, quia nec obitus
eius uspiam legitur, dum tamen reperiatur eius sepulcrum, ut aliqui dicunt,
in ualle Iosaphat.' = 'In particular, no text teaches that Mary was killed by
the punishment of the sword, for her death is recorded nowhere, whereas,
as some say, her sepulchre is found in the valley of Josaphat.' Clayton (note
25), 13, comments that 'the legend of Mary's tomb in the valley of
Josaphat...seems to have arisen in the mid-fifth century and was the result
of locating in this valley the house in which Mary was said to have lived
with Joseph. The house was gradually transformed into her sepulchre, or
the two were regarded as being in close proximity to each other.' A cavern
between Saint Stephen's Gate and the Mount of Olives in Jerusalem is still
identified as the Virgin's tomb. See Jerome Murphy O'Connor, *The Holy
Land* (Oxford 1998) 130.
46. Adamnan († c. 704), *De locis sanctis*, ed. and trans. D. Meehan, *Adamnan's
De locis sanctis*, Scriptores Latini Hiberniae 3 (Dublin 1958) 58: Sed de eodem
sepulchro quo modo uel in quo tempore aut a quibus personis sanctum
corpusculum eius sit sublatum uel in quo loco resurrectionem expectat
ullus, ut refert, pro certo scire potest.

The anglo-saxon monk Bede († 735) wrote with some reser-
vations that, because she was 'truly full of grace', she may have
been raised up to heaven as once she had been 'raised from
earthly to heavenly desires . . . and afterwards sanctified'.[47]
Another Anglo-Saxon, a nun living in Germany, echoed the
bishop of Tours' opinion that Mary's body had been miraculously taken 'from the hands of the apostles and carried' to
heaven by angels.[48] By the time the Cistercians appeared on
the scene four centuries later, differences of opinion still ex-
isted as to whether Mary's body as well as her soul had been
assumed into heaven,[49] but by then no one doubted that she
does somehow dwell in God's presence, and the focus of disagreement had shifted to whether 'the blessed Virgin under-
went the vexation of the flesh by dying' before being taken
up.[50]

   Back in the seventh century, Isidore of Seville, in his much-
used encyclopaedic compendium of all human knowledge,
had provided future generations with the etymology of Mary's
name—*stella maris*, star of the sea[51]—along with a list of doctri-
nally acceptable titles, among them: 'rod of Jesse', 'garden enclosed', 'sealed fountain', and 'Virgin before giving birth, Virgin after giving birth'.[52] Like the Latin Fathers on whom he
drew, he exalted her as the type of the Church[53] and the head
of female virgins—Christ being the head of male virgins.[54]

---

47. Sermon One for Advent 1.3; translated Lawrence T. Martin and Dom
David Hurst, *Bede the Venerable: Homilies on the Gospels*, Book One, CS 110
(Kalamazoo, 1991) 21.
48. *The Hodoeporicon of St Willibald by* Huneberc (alt. Hygeburg); *Vita Willibaldi*,
ed. Holder-Egger, MGH SS 15/1: 907-98; translated C. H. Talbot, *The Anglo-
Saxon Missionares in Germany* (London: Sheed and Ward, 1954) 166. Cumque
illi .xi. Apostoli tollentes corpus sanctae Mariae portauerunt illum de
Hierusalem. . . .
49. E.g. Ratramnus of Corbie, *De assumptione* 8-9: 112-113. 8.
50. E.g. Peter Damian (†1072), *Opuscula* 55.1; PL 145:800-801.
51. *Etymologiae* 7.10.1: PL 82:289; Cf. Ps-Jerome, *Breviarium in Psalmos*; PL
26:873B; Bede, *In Lucam* 1:CCSL 120:31.
52. Isidore, *De ortu et obitu patrum* 111; PL 83:148.
53. *Allegoriae* 139; PL 83:117.
54. *De ecclesiasticis officiis* 2.18; PL 83:804.

Conceding the absence of any documentation, he doubted that she had been martyred. Another seventh-century spanish bishop, in addition to invoking her aid,[55] and composing a number of antiphons and homilies in honor of her Assumption,[56] translated a popular greek legend about a certain Theophilus who had been rescued from a faustlike pact with the devil by Mary's intervention.

The Monastic Model

Monks through the ages tended to regard Mary as the embodiment of monastic virtues and a precursor of that freedom from sin which will someday be ours in Christ. Bede refers to her in a homily for the Feast of the Purification as 'God's blessed mother and a perpetual virgin' who was 'by a singular privilege above the law', and has given us 'an example of humility'.[57] Convinced that Mary had been sanctified while still in her mother's womb, he was also sure that, at the moment she conceived Christ, she had been purified from original sin by the Holy Spirit—all of which fitted the augustinian theological conviction that 'the heat of concupiscence does not exist where the Holy Spirit casts his shade'.[58] Christ's first salvific act, Bede further believed, had been to redeem his Mother, 'who was not saved from iniquity by any of her own preceding merits, but redeemed by the blood of Christ'.[59]

Because the Word Incarnate received his human 'flesh from the sanctified flesh of the Virgin',[60] moreover, a carolingian monk, Paschasius Radbertus, reasoned, Christ's own freedom from the sin that infects all humankind must depend on his

55. Ildefons of Toldeo (†667), *De virginitate perpetua sanctae Mariae*, 1–cited Edmund Bishop, *Liturgica Historica* (Oxford: Clarendon) 1970) 176.
56. PL 95:1565-1574   57. *Sermon for the Purification*; CS 110: 180.
58. Bede, *In Lucam* 1:CCCM 120:36. Erit in te conceptio, libido non erit. Concupiscentiae no erit aestus ubi umbram fecit Spiritus sanctus.
59. Bede, *In Lucam* 1; 36.
60. *De partu virginis*, CCCM 56C:55: ex sanctificata carne uirginis Verbum carnem.

mother's sinlessness at the moment of his conception.[61] 'Although she was herself conceived and born of the flesh of sin', he wrote, she did not pass that flesh of sin on to her Son. If she had *not* been 'sanctified and cleansed' by the Holy Spirit, Radbertus asked, how could she *not* have transmitted her sin to her Son?[62]

As a mark of the veneration due the woman who, by a 'singular prerogative'[63] gave birth with neither pain nor loss of virginity and who now sees God face to face, a Mass in Mary's honor came to be celebrated on all Saturdays on which no other commemoration fell. [64]   This parallel to her Son's worship on Sunday, Peter Damien in the eleventh century explained, is based on the scriptural revelation that God rested on the sixth day, and Mary is the 'home which Wisdom built and in it ... as in an utterly sacred bed, He took his rest.'[65]

By the first half of the eleventh century, as veneration for the Mother of Christ unfolded from liturgical feasts and the musings of monks, the pious made personal vows of homage and vassalage to her[66] and the learned composed new hymns, sequences, and homilies in her honor.[67]   Among them were marian antiphons still sung today. Legend has it that the *Alma Redemptoris Mater* was composed by a crippled monk on the island of Reichenau;[68] the *Salve Regina*, which later came to be expressly associated with the Cistercians, was added around 1035 to the repertoire of the great abbey of Cluny, the liturgi-

61. Paschasius Radbertus, *Cogitis me* (c. 860); PL 120:1371-1372.

62. *De partu virginis;* CCCM 56C:52: Alioquin, si non eodem Spiritu Sancto sanctificata est et emundata, quomodo caro eius non caro peccati fuit? Et si caro eius de massa primae praeuaricationis venit, quomodo Christus *Verbum caro* sine peccato fuit, qui de carne peccati carnem assumpsit....

63. Guitmond of Aversa, *De corpore et sanguinis Christi veritate in eucharistia* 1; PL 149:1443.

64. As mandated in tenth-century England by the *Regularis concordia;* PL 137:483C.

65. Peter Damian, *De bono suffragiorum* 4; PL 145:565-566: ...quia sapientia domum aedificavit atque in ea ... velut in sacratissimo lectulo requievit.

66. E.g. Abbot Odilo of Cluny (†1049) *Vita Odilonis* 2.1; PL 142:915.

67. E.g. Bishop Fulbert of Chartres (†1028).

68. Probably by Herman the Lame (†1054) at his monastery on the island

cal pacesetter of Europe. Parents committed their children to her protection[69] and entreated her help when they fell ill.[70] Prayers addressed to her were circulated among friends,[71] and in many parts of Europe an Office of the Virgin was being recited daily by layfolk as well as monks.[72]

By the eleventh century, too, the Virgin Mother was being regarded not only as unique among women and, in fact, among all created beings, even angels, because of her 'singular privilege of merits', but as capable of ensuring that these merits are applied to 'our debts'.[73] Two new marian feasts were introduced early in that century, again from the east . One commemorated her Presentation in the Temple (21 November), mirroring the feast of the Christ's Presentation. The other, corresponding to the Annunciation, celebrated the Virgin's Conception (8 December). While the latter had been on the calendar of the eastern Church since the year 600, in the Latin Church it seems to have been celebrated uniquely in the south of England.[74] The conquering Normans removed it as an innovation unfounded in Scripture or tradi-

---

of Reichenau in Lake Constance—which by the late tenth century possessed a translation of greek sermons on the Dormition. See Chrysogonus Waddell, 'Blessed Herman and the *Alma Redemptoris mater*', *Liturgy OCSO* 27:2-3 (1993) 85-95: 'Apodictic proof that Bl. Hermann was the author of this exquisite marian antiphon is, as a matter of fact, non-existent' (85). Other scholars, in fact, dispute his authorship.

69. E.g. Guibert of Nogent, *De vita sua* 1.3; PL 156:842.

70 See Ronald C. Finucane, *The Rescue of the Innocents: Endangered Children in Medieval Miracles* (New York : St. Martin's Press, 1997).

71. See, for a late eleventh-century example, *The Prayers and Meditations of Saint Anselm*, translated by Benedicta Ward (Penguin, 1979).

72. E.g. the Life of Margaret of Scotland, *Symeonis Dunelmensis Opera* (1857) 51,247-8. Clayton (above, n. 25, pp. 65-67, cites evidence from Verdun, Augsburg, and England.

73. Peter Damian (†1072), *Carmina* B.44.9—cited by Pelikan (above, n. 35), 161.

74. Clayton (above n.25), 50. Whether it was known earlier at Naples, and whether it had still earlier, perhaps as early as the ninth century, arrived in Ireland is still apparently under debate. See P. Grosjean, 'Notes d'hagiographie celtique: la prétendue fête de la Conception dans les églises celtiques' in *Analecta Bollandiana* 61 (1943) 91-95; and Edmund Bishop, *Liturgica Historica* (Oxford: Clarendon, 1970), Chapter X, pp. 238-259.

tion, and when its observance began filtering into France it
was challenged on the same grounds by Bernard of Clairvaux.[75]
Before we look more closely at this feast, however, we need
to pause briefly at Canterbury to meet the enormously influ-
ential second norman archbishop, Saint Anselm.

A scholar and former monk of Bec, Anselm voiced a very
personal devotion to the Virgin in his meditations,[76] calling
her the 'gateway of life, door of salvation, way of reconciliation, approach to recovery' and entreating the prayers of the
'woman uniquely to be wondered at and to be wondered at
for your uniqueness.'[77] This same deep respect is echoed in
his theology. The Blessed Virgin Mary, he wrote, enjoys a
purity 'than which, under God, nothing greater can be
thought.'[78] As the bearer of the Redeemer, she is the means
by which 'the elements are renewed, hell is redeemed, demons are trampled down and men are saved, even fallen angels are restored to their place.'[79] She is

the mother of the Creator and Saviour,
by whose sanctity my sins are purged,
by whose integrity incorruptibility is given me.[80]

Even while he believed that 'Nothing equals Mary, nothing but God is greater than Mary',[81] Anselm never wavered in
pointing out that her holiness and the help she provides depend absolutely on Christ and her unique relationship with
'the salvation born of your fruitfulness.'

75. Letter 174; *Sancti Bernardi Opera* 7:388-392.
76. Beautifully translated by Benedicta Ward, *The Prayers and Meditations of Saint Anselm* (Penguin books, 1979).
77. *Oratio* 7; F. S. Schmitt ed, *S. Anselmi Cantuariensis Archiepiscopi Opera* Omnia, vol. 7 (Edinburgh 1946). Translated Ward, *Prayers and Meditations* (above, n. 74). Cited hereafter as 3 BVM.
78. Anselm, *De conceptu virginis* 18; Schmitt 2:159.
79. 3 BVM, lines 152-153.
80. 3 BVM = *Oratio* 7; Schmitt 3:19: matri creatoris et salvatoris mei per cujus sanctitatem peccata mea purgantur, per suius integritatem mihi incor-ruptabilitatis donatur ....
81. 3 BVM, lines 185-187.

God created all things, and Mary gave birth to God.
God who made all things made himself of Mary,
and thus he refashioned everything he had made.[82]

Anselm's influence over later theology was enormous. So too was that of his long-time companion and eventual biographer, an anglo-saxon monk named Eadmer († c. 1128). In addition to his account of the saintly archbishop's life and death, he composed a 'charming and naïve, yet substantial little treatise,'[83] as part of a campaign to have the feast of the Virgin's Conception restored to the Canterbury calendar. In earlier times, this feast day had been celebrated by those of 'purer simplicity and quite humble devotion', Eadmer complained, but then it had been suppressed by those having 'greater learning and spurning the simplicity of the poor'.[84]   He justified the commemoration on the evidence of the text 'where the spirit of the Lord is, there is freedom,'[85] reasoning that Mary, 'the court of appeal for all sinners, was therefore free from slavery to all sin.'[86]   Eadmer could not have been unaware of Archbishop Anselm's contrary opinion that 'the virgin herself, from whom [Christ] sprang, was conceived in iniquity, and in sin did her mother bear her, since she had sinned in Adam, in whom all sinned.'[87]

82. 3 BVM, 188-194.
83. E. D. O'Connor, *New Catholic Encyclopedia* 7:380.
84. Eadmer, *Tractatus de conceptione B. Mariae Virginis*; PL 159:301: . . . ab eis praecipue in quibus pura simplicitas et humilior in Deum vigebat devotio. At ubi et major scientia et praepollens examinatio rerum mentes quorumdam imbuit et erexit, eadem solemnitatem, spreta pauperum simplicitate, de medio sustulit; et eam quasi ratione vacantem redegit in nihilum.   85. 2 Cor 3:17.
86. *Tractatus de conceptione*; PL 159:305B: . . . a servitute igitur peccatorum libera fuit, quae omnium peccatorum propitiatori aula. . . .
87. *Cur Deus Homo* II.16; Schmitt 2:116: Nam licet ipsa hominis conceptio munda sit et absque carnalis delectationis peccato, virgo tamen ipsa unde assumptus est, in iniquitatibus *concepta est* et in peccatis concepit *eam* mater *eius, et cum originali peccato nata est, quoniam et ipsa in Adam peccavit*, in quo omnes peccaverunt. (Psalm 51:5; Romans 5:12).

Eadmer, like generations of monks before him, cautiously professed himself unwilling to dissent from the truth of the catholic and universal Church,[88] yet he pointed out that if Jeremiah and John the Baptist could be sanctified in the womb, which on explicit scriptural evidence no one doubted, then

> Who would dare say that the unique propi-
> tiation of the whole world and tenderest
> couch of the Son of Almighty God was de-
> prived at the outset of her conception of the
> enlightening grace of the Holy Spirit?...[God]
> clearly could do it, and he willed [to do it]. So
> if he willed it, he did it.[89]

As R. W. Southern observes, 'Eadmer here followed Anselm in method, and went beyond him in doctrine ....'[90] Later generations attached Anselm's more authoritative name to Eadmer's treatise without always adverting to the discrepancy in the two men's opinions. The consequences of that confusion, however, lie outside the scope of our story.

By the time Anselm died in 1109, familiarity with the apocryphal tradition and with liturgical festivals, intensified by crusader contacts with biblical sites and eastern customs, issued in a new marian literature which reflected a vibrant affection for Mary. 'Quite suddenly toward the end of the eleventh century,' as Southern writes, '... large numbers of miracle stories of the Virgin began to appear'[91] and to be read

---

88. *Tractatus de conceptione*, PL 159:305.
89. *Ibid.* 305B, D.: ... quis dicere audeat singulare totius saeculi propitiatorium, ac ilii Dei omnipoentis dulcissimum reclinatorium, mox in suae conceptionis exordio Spiritu sancti gratiae illustratione destitutum? ... potuit plane, et voluit; si igitur voluit, fecit.
90. R. W. Southern, *Saint Anselm. Portrait in a Landscape.* (Cambridge University Press) 433.
91. R. W. Southern, *The Making of the Middle Ages* (above, n. 31) 248. On the textual history of *The Apocryphal Gospels of Mary in Anglo-Saxon England*, see the recent book of that title by Mary Clayton (Cambridge: University Press, 1999).

at all levels of society. An increasingly active and affluent merchant class looked to her, a carpenter's wife and queen of heaven, for inspiration and intercession. Cathedrals and parish churches as well as monasteries were increasingly dedicated to her patronage; [92] even great churches dedicated to others saint frequently had 'Lady chapels' behind the high altar.

Castle and Cloister

As the twelfth century began, knights, scholars, and monks all continued to move within a very masculine world. Yet in one male stronghold, the castle, a growing cult of courtly love increasingly set women at either extreme of the moral scale: oversexed seductresses to be resisted on pain of damnation or pure ladies to be given homage, defended, and entreated for favors. The long familiar typology of Eve and Mary provided a paradigm: 'The one was the handmaid of seduction, the other of propitiation. The one gave birth to lies, the other brought redemption.'[93] That noblest, most gracious, chaste and clement of all ladies, the mother of the Lord of heaven and earth, was believed to provide the most potent and most enduring protection possible for sinners. 'Like the rain,' Southern writes, 'this protective power of the Virgin falls on the just and the unjust alike—provided only that they have entered the circle of her allegiance.'[94]

While many young nobles were riding east to seek their fortunes in the sands of the Levant, some of their kinsmen back home were surging in record numbers into newly founded cloisters or schools, sparking both theological in-

92. See, for example, Allison Binns, *Dedications of Monastic Houses in England and Wales, 1066-1216* (Woodbridge – Wolfeboro, NH: Boydell Press, 1989).
93. Bernard of Clairvaux, Sermon on the Octave of the Assumption 2; SBOp 5:263: Illa enim ministra seductionis, haec propitiationis; illa suggessit praevaricationem, haec ingessit redemptionem.
94. *The Making of the Middle Ages* (above, n. 31), 248.

quiry and contemplative reflection. In his overtly marian exegesis of the Song of Songs,[95] one benedictine abbot spoke of the 'utterly pure matter from which the holy Wisdom of God' had became man.[96] Another 'black monk' early in the century[97] referred to Mary as 'my sister, coheir in the glory of the Father, spouse of the Father'[98] and, with no immodesty, interpreted her breasts as humility and chastity 'nourishing little ones in faith' and again as the active and contemplative life styles.[99] The daily recitation in many places[100] of the combined salutations of Gabriel and Elizabeth— *Hail Mary, full of grace. The Lord is with you. Blessed are you among women and blessed is the fruit of your womb*—accustomed people to entreating her aid and, in a theological climate which equated grace with the remission of sins,[101] inexorably set some minds meandering to logical inferences.

---

[95] In what some scholars date as the first marian exegesis the Song; see John Van Engen, *Rupert of Deutz* 275-282, 291-98; and F. Ohly, *Hohenliedstudien. Grundzüge einer Geschichte der Hohenliedauslegun des Abendlandes bis zum 1200* (Wiesbaden 1958) 121-135.

[96] Rupert of Deutz, *Commentaria in Canticum canticorum*, ed H. Haacke, CCCM 26:12: *tota omnino munda materia, de qua sancta Dei sapientia....*

[97] On the dating, see Valerie Flint, 'The Chronology of the Works of Honorius Augustodunensis,' *Revue Bénédictine* 82 (1972) 215-242.

[98] Honorius Augustodunensis, *Sigillum Beatae Mariae* 5, trans. Amelia Carr, *The Seal of Blessed* Mary (Toronto: Peregrina, 1991) 69.

[99] Ibid. 4; p. 67.

[100] Lk 1:28, 42. Baldwin, the cistercian abbot of Ford and later archbishop of Canterbury, bears witness to the daily recitation of the Hail Mary in its scriptural form in *Sermo* 13.45; CCCM 99:206 = Tractate 7. Cp. translation by D. N. Bell in CF 38:209.

[101] *Inter plurima: Glossa Ordinaria*; PL 114:559D.: Gratia Dei est remissio peccatorum. Lanfranc of Bec, *Epistola B. Pauli apostoli ad Romanos, glossula interhjecta B. Lanfranci explanata* 1.9; PL 150:107B. Robert of Melun: *Commentary on Romans* 1.7; SSL 18 (Louvain 1938) 16. William of Saint Thierry, *Expositio in Epistola ad Romanos* ad 1.5 and ad 1.7; CCCM 86 (1989) 9, 10. Peter Lombard, *Commentary on Romans*; PL 191:1316B. I am indebted for these citations to Dr Aage Rydstrøm-Paulsen.

The 'New Monastery'

Perhaps the most masculine of all medieval enclaves was the cistercian monastery, the gates of which no woman might enter.[102] Yet within its walls the Mother of Christ embodied the very virtues of humility and obedience which the monks endeavored to acquire, and she brought to perfection the love of God which they defined as the very essence of their way of life:

> Our order is an awareness of our need.
> It is humbleness.
> It is poverty, freely accepted,
> obedience, peace, joy in the Holy Spirit . . . .
> Our order means learning to be silent,
> to fast, to keep watch, to pray, to work with our hands,
> and above all to cling to that most excellent way
> which is love. [103]

Believing that 'perfection of the human person is likeness to God',[104] these Cistercians hoped by their disciplined obedience and God-directed love to be re-formed to the image of Christ and so trans-formed from the deformity of sin 'into the likeness of God which may be called not just likeness, but unity of spirit, by which the human person becomes one with God'.[105] What better patron could they choose than the

102. *Capitula XVII* and *XVIII*, attached to the *Exordium cistercii* and *Summa cartae caritatis*, ed. Chrysogonus Waddell, *Narrative and Legislative Sources from Early Cîteaux* Studia et Documenta 9 (Cîteaux: Commentarii Cistercienses, 1999) 411.
103. Bernard, Letter 142; PL 182:297: Ordo noster abjectio est, humilitas est, voluntaria paupertas est, obedientia, pax, gaudium in Spiritu sancto. Ordo noster est esse sub magistro, sub abbate, sub regula, sub disciplina. Ordo noster est studere silentio, exerceri jejuniis, vigiliis, orationibus, opere manuum; et super omnia, excellentiorem viam tenere, quae est charitas.
104. William of St Thierry, *The Golden Epistle* 16.269; PL 184:348: Et haec hominis est perfectio, similitudo Dei. A translation by Theodore Berkeley appears in *William of St Thierry: The Golden Epistle*, CF 12:97.
105. *The Golden Epistle* 16.262; PL 184: 349: ut non jam similitudo, sed unitas spiritus nominetur; cum fit homo unum cum Deo. Cp. CF 12:95-96.

woman who in humility, faith, obedience, and love had given
herself wholly up to God and whose body God had shared?
The church of the 'New Monastery' at Cîteaux was dedicated
to her honor, as were the churches of its many rapidly prolif-
erating daughter houses.[106] Cistercian abbots meditated in
private, and on appropriate feast days preached to their monks
on Mary, the model of christian and therefore monastic perfection. The Advent season moved them to reflect on judgement and fallen humankind's need for a Saviour, and therefore on the indispensable role of his mother. The Feast of the
Purification reminded them of her humility and of the sac-
rifices she had been called to make. The Feast of Assumption
drew them to meditate on the woman who, having risen
before us to eternal life is our pledge of resurrection and perfection in Christ.[107]

None of the Cistercians spoke with more moving eloquence than Bernard, the first abbot of Clairvaux, († 1153).
His homilies on Blessed Mary have been read and repeated so
frequently over the centuries that popular histories have
sometimes erroneously laid the twelfth-century surge of
marian devotion at his door. Yet, as we have seen, Bernard was
neither the first nor the last to hymn the praises of Mary, the
unique mother and unique bride of Christ.[108]

From Norway to the Mediterranean, from Ireland to the
Holy Land, men—and very soon women—offered their lives
to Christ in unprecedented numbers in cistercian abbeys.
Of all the homilies preached at the over six hundred medieval cistercian abbeys, few have survived and fewer still have
been translated. Yet even the small sampling included in this
book gives some idea of the chorus of praise which rose to
heaven from the choirstalls and *scriptoria* of the White Monks.
From France, the cistercian homeland, we hear the mellifluous and charismatic spokesman of cistercian renewal, Ber-

---

106. See above, page v. *Exordium cistercii* VIII; *Narrative and Legislative Texts
from Early Cîteaux*, ed. Chrysogonus Waddell (Cîteaux 1999) 187.
107. Aelred, *Sermo* 20.32; CCCM 2a:163.
108. Aelred, *Sermo* 20.6; CCCM 2a:156.

nard of Clairvaux; that of his friend, William of Saint Thierry, who came late to cistercian life from the Benedictines († 1148); and that of his secretary, Geoffrey of Auxerre († after 1188), who abandoned the schools for the cloister. We listen as well to two of his erstwhile monks: Guerric, abbot of Igny near the French royal city of Reims († 1157), and Amadeus of Lausanne, bishop of what is today a Swiss city. From England, where the first cistercian abbey was founded in 1128, we share the meditations of two Yorkshire abbots Aelred of Rievaulx († 1178) and Stephen of Sawley († 1252). To their insights we add those of Gilbert, abbot of Swineshead 'in Hoyland' († 1172); and of John and Baldwin of Forde Abbey in Dorset. Isaac of Stella († 1167), an Englishman who spent most of his life in France, and Adam, abbot of Perseigne († c. 1221) in Normandy, remind us of the ease with which educated persons communicated by the common use of Latin. From further east and slightly later, we catch the sound of the feminine voice of Gertrud, one of the remarkable nuns of the abbey of Helfta and one of many nuns who followed the cistercian way of life, whether or not the General Chapter recognized them as officially within the Order. Divided in place and even in time, they all chant together, as in a monastic choir, the praises of Mary Most Holy, the Mother of Mercy who is 'our life, our sweetness, and our hope.'[109]

---

109. From the *Salve Regina*.

Mary
Most Holy

Meditations and Reflections
by Cistercian Monks and Nuns
of the Twelfth and Thirteenth Centuries

The Virgin's Name was Mary

In the sixth month the angel Gabriel was sent from God to a city of Galilee named Nazareth, to a virgin betrothed to a man whose name was Joseph, of the house of David; and the virgin's name was Mary. And he came to her and said, 'Hail, Full of Grace, the Lord is with you!' But she was greatly troubled at the saying, and considered in her mind what sort of greeting this might be. And the angel said to her, 'Do not be afraid, Mary, for you have found grace with God. And behold, you will conceive in your womb and bear a son, and you shall call his name Jesus. He will be great, and will be called the Son of the Most High; and the Lord God will give to him the throne of his father David, and he will reign over the house of Jacob for ever; and of his kingdom there will be no end.' And Mary said to the angel, 'How shall this be, for I do not know a man?' And the angel said to her, 'The Holy Spirit will come upon you, and the power of the Most High will overshadow you; therefore the child to be born will be called holy, the Son of God. And behold, your kinswoman Elizabeth in her old age has also conceived a son; and this is the sixth month with her who was called barren. For with God nothing will be impossible.' And Mary said, 'Behold the handmaid of the Lord; be it unto me according to your word.' And the angel departed from her.

Luke 2:6-7

With a salutation
our salvation begins
and the commencement of our reconciliation
is consecrated
by a proclamation of peace.

The herald of salvation and messenger of peace
was sent from God
and came to the Virgin.

And this lover of virginity greeted her
with a strange new greeting
which never
—from all eternity until that moment—
had been heard,
and so conferred upon her
at one and the same time
both the favor of a new greeting
and the acclaim of a new commendation.

For a woman to be greeted by an angel
is indeed new and rare!
Although Hagar and the wife of Manoah enjoyed
seeing an angel
and speaking with him,
the angel did not greet them.[1]

Yet now
a woman is greeted by an angel.

Now
the time draws near
when women may be greeted by the Lord himself,
saying to them, 'All hail'.[2]

Baldwin *of* Forde[3]

[1] Gen 21:17; Jg 13:9-20
[2] Mt 28.9
[3] Tractate 7

The angel Gabriel

is entrusted with a novel task
and the Virgin
manifests a new virtue:
she is honored by a novel salutation.

The ancient curse of women[1]
is removed.
The new mother
receives a new blessing.[2]

She is filled with grace
which knows nothing of fleshly desire,
so that,
by the Spirit's coming upon her,
she who refuses to give herself to a man
may give birth
to the Son of the Most High.

Bernard *of* Clairvaux[3]

[1] Gen 3:1
[2] Lk 1:28.
[3] Sermon Two for the Feast of the Annunciation, 1

At the time the angel came
perhaps
Mary was holding in her hands [the text of] Isaiah,
perhaps
she was then studying
the prophecy which declares:
Behold a virgin shall conceive and bear a son
and his name will be called
Emmanuel.[1]

At this moment, I think,
these [words of the] Scriptures
were producing a very appealing conflict
in her heart.

When she read
that it was to come to pass
that a certain virgin
would give birth to the Son of God,
then secretly
and with some fear
—I think—
she longed
that she might be that virgin.

But at the same time
she considered herself utterly unworthy
of being granted such a privilege.

Charity conflicted with fear,
devotion with humility.

At one moment
she almost despaired
through overwhelming fear;
at the next,
through the overwhelming desire
she drew from it,
she could not but hope.

First, devotion moved her to presume to it,
but then her great humility moved her to hesitate.

It was then,
when she was hesitating,
wavering,
longing,
that *the angel came in to her and said:*
Hail, full of grace.[2]

Aelred of Rievaulx[3]

[1] Is 7:14
[2] Lk 1:28
[3] Sermon 9.19-20: On the Feast of the Annunciation

Reflect
on the sort of gifts
the Son of God sent
to his bride.

At the moment there come to mind
the gifts which Abraham's son sent
by his father's servant
to Rebecca, his bride.

Mary, like Rachel,
was a very beautiful virgin
who had never known a man.[1]

Abraham's servant found her by the water.
There he spoke to her
and there he gave her the gifts.[2]

Our loveliest virgin
—of whom I am speaking—
freely dwelt by spiritual waters,
that is, by the sacred Scriptures.

To these waters she had frequent recourse.
So, with the Prophet, she could say:
He leads me beside refreshing waters.[3]

There
she was found by the angel,
the servant of Abraham
—not the earthly and mortal [Abraham]
but the heavenly and eternal.

Accordingly,
the Evangelist says:
The angel came in to her and said:
Hail, full of grace.[4]

Where was it
that he *came into her?*
Doubtless there
where she had hidden herself
from the vanities of the world and its cares.

She had gone into her private chamber
and closed the door
and was praying to her Father
in secret.[5]

She was *drawing waters*
for herself
in joy from the fountain of the Saviour,[6]
that is, from the sacred Scriptures,
where she had read about
both the virgin's giving birth
and the Saviour's coming.

Aelred of Rievaulx [7]

[1] Gen 24:16
[2] Gen 24: 13-22
[3] Ps 22 [23]:2
[4] Lk 1:28
[5] Cf. Mt 6:6
[6] Is 12:3
[7] Sermon 9:17-18: On the Feast of the Annunciation

*The angel was sent
to a Virgin.*[1]

A virgin in her body
a virgin in her spirit
a virgin by profession
a virgin such as the Apostle describes:
holy in spirit and body.[2]

Now was this Virgin discovered at the last minute
as if by chance.
She was chosen ages ago.
The Most High foreknew her
and prepared her for himself.

She was preserved
by the angels
prefigured
by the patriarchs
promised
by the prophets.

Search the Scriptures
and verify what I am saying.

Bernard *of* Clairvaux[3]

[1] Lk 1:26-27
[2] 1 Cor 7:34
[3] Homily Two in Praise of the Blessed Virgin Mary, 4

So that she might conceive
and give birth
to
the Holy of Holies[1]
she was made holy in her body
by the gift of virginity.
And to become holy in spirit too
she accepted
the gift of humility.

This queenly maiden
—adorned with the jewels of these virtues
radiant with this perfect beauty
of spirit and body
renowned in the assembly of the Most High
for her loveliness and her beauty—
so ravished the eyes of all the heavenly citizens
that the heart of the King himself
desired her beauty
and sent down from on high
a heavenly messenger
to her.

And this is what the Evangelist is telling us here
when he states that an angel was sent
from God to a virgin.

He says
from God to a virgin
from the highest to the humble
from the Master to the handmaiden
from the Creator to the creature.

How kind God is!
How matchless is the Virgin!

Bernard *of* Clairvaux [2]

[1] Cf Dan 9:24
[2] Homily Two in Praise of the Blessed Virgin Mary, 2

The Lord is with you.

Is there any special glory in her being told
The Lord is with you?

After all,
the angel said to Gideon
The Lord is with you, o strongest of men.[1]

And the Psalmist says
The Lord of hosts is with us.[2]

And Christ says to us
*Behold, I am with you always
even to the end of the world.*[3]

And Isaiah says of Christ,
*They shall call his name Emmanuel
God with us.'*[4]

But he had prefaced what he was going to say with
Behold, a virgin shall conceive
and shall bear a son
and they shall call his name Emmanuel.[5]

How could he come to us
to be with us
unless he comes to the Virgin?

To her
he came first
so as to be with her
and in her
and from her
so that
through her
he should be in us
since he is the God of Jacob, our protector.[6]

The reason that the God of Jacob
took our nature
from her
was so that he might always be
with us
saying
My delight is to be with the children of men.[7]

Baldwin *of* Ford[8]

[1] Jdg 6:12
[2] Ps 45:8
[3] Mt 28:20
[4] Is 7:14
[5] *Ibid.*
[6] Ps 45:12
[7] Pr 8:31
[8] Tractate 7

But when she heard this
she was troubled at the saying
and pondered what sort of greeting this might be.[1]

It is usual for virgins
—those who really are virgins—
always to be timid
and never to feel safe.
They are so constantly on guard against danger
that they easily take fright
because they know
that they carry a precious treasure
in an earthen vessel[2]

13

That explains
why Mary was troubled
by what the angel said to her.

She was troubled,
but not distressed.

It is written:
*I am troubled and do not speak
but I consider the days of old
I remember the years long past.*[3]

And so it was with Mary.

She was troubled
she did not speak
but she pondered
what sort of greeting this might be.[4]

That she should be troubled
is only virginal reserve.

Not to be distressed
shows courage.

That she was silent and pondered
shows prudence.

But she pondered what sort of greeting this might be.

Bernard *of* Clairvaux [5]

[1] Lk 1:29
[2] 2 Cor 4:7
[3] Ps 77:4-5
[4] Lk 1:29
[5] Homily Three in Praise of the Blessed Virgin Mary, 9

Virgin,

you have heard what will happen.
You have heard how it will happen.
You have a double reason for astonishment and
rejoicing.

Rejoice, o Daughter of Sion,
and be exceeding glad, Daughter of Jerusalem.[1]

And since you have heard joyous and glad tidings,
let us hear that joyous reply we long for,
so that broken bones may rejoice.[2]
You have heard what is to happen, I repeat,
and you have believed.
Believe also the way you have heard it is to happen.

You have heard that you will conceive and bear a son.
You have heard that it will be by the Holy Spirit,
and not by a man.

The angel is waiting
for your reply.
It is time for him to return
to the One who sent him.

We, too, are waiting
for this merciful word,
my lady.
We who are miserably weighed down
under a sentence of condemnation.
The price of our salvation
is being offered to you.

If you consent,
we shall immediately be set free.
In the eternal Word of God
we all have been made
and look,
we are dying.[3]

In your brief reply
we shall be restored
and so brought back to life.

Doleful Adam and his unhappy offspring,
exiled from Paradise,
implore you, kind virgin,
to give this answer.
David asks it.
Abraham asks it.
All the other holy patriarchs,
your very own fathers,
beg it of you,
as do those now dwelling in the region of the
shadow of death.[4]

For it
the whole world is waiting,
bowed down at your feet.
And rightly so
because on your answer depends
the comfort of the afflicted
the redemption of captives
the deliverance of the damned
the salvation of all the sons of Adam
your whole race.

Give your answer quickly, my Virgin.
My Lady, say this word
which earth and hell and heaven itself are waiting for.

The very King and Lord of all,
who has so desired your beauty,[5]
is waiting anxiously for your answer and assent,
by which he proposes to save the world.[6]

Him, whom you pleased by your silence,
you will now please even more
by your word.

He calls out to you from heaven:
*O fair among women,
let me hear your voice.*[7]
If you let him hear your voice,
he will let you see our salvation.

Is this not what you have been waiting for,
what you have been weeping for
and sighing after,
day and night,
in your prayers?

What then?
Are you the one who was promised,
or must we look for another?[8]
No,
it is you
and no one else.

You, I say, are the one we were promised,
you are the one we are expecting,
you are the one we have longed for,
in whom your holy ancestor Jacob
—as he was approaching death—
put all his hope of eternal life,
saying:
I shall wait for your salvation, Lord.[9]

You are she
in whom and by whom
God our King himself
before all ages
decided to work out our salvation
in the midst of the earth.[10]

Why hope from another
for what is now being offered to you?
Why expect from another woman
what will soon be shown forth through you,
if only you will consent and say the word?

So answer the angel quickly
or rather, through the angel,
answer God.

Only say the word
and receive the Word.
Give yours
and conceive God's.[11]

Breathe one fleeting word
and embrace the everlasting Word.

Why do you delay?
Why be afraid?

Believe,
give praise,
and receive.

Let humility take courage
and shyness confidence.
This is not the moment for virginal simplicity
to forget prudence.

In this circumstance alone,
O prudent Virgin,
do not fear presumptuousness,
for if your reserve pleased by its silence,
now much more must your goodness speak.
Blessed Virgin,
open your heart to faith,
your lips to consent,
and your womb to your Creator.

Behold, the long-desired of all nations[12]
is standing at the door and knocking.[13]
Get up, run, open!
Get up by faith,
run by prayer,
open by consent!

Behold, she says,
I am the handmaiden of the Lord.
Being it unto me according to your word.[14]

Bernard *of* Clairvaux [15]

[1] Zech 9:9
[2] Ps 51:8
[3] 2 Cor 6:9
[4] Is 9:2
[5] Ps 45:11
[6] Jn 3:17
[7] Sg 1:7
[8] Mt 11:3

[9] Gen 49:18
[10] Ps 74:12
[11] Cf. Jas 1:21
[12] Hag 2:8
[13] Rev 2:20
[14] Lk 1:38
[15] Homily Four in Praise of the Blessed Virgin Mary, 8

Upon whom shall I rest
says the Lord,
if not with the humble
and the quiet
and those who fear my words? [1]

/3

'Upon whom shall I rest
if not with the humble?
In all I sought rest
but I found it
with a humble handmaid.'

No one was found like her [2]
in the grace of humility;
therefore all the fullness of the godhead [3] rested
even in bodily form
in this fullness of humility.

Yet it rested in another way
in the Son
for although the Mother
was very humble
the Son was far more humble.

Guerric of Igny [4]

[1] Is 66:2
[2] Cf. Si 44:20
[3] Cf Col 2:9
[4] Sermon 40.4: Third Sermon for the Feast of the Assumption

Perplexed and wondering
at Gabriel's extraordinary and fitting greeting,
she did not immediately speak.

She thought
she deliberated
she waited
until the angel
proceeding with the mission he had begun
added to what he had first said
more important things.

At length,
answering him with a reverent question,
she asked
How can this be?[1]

She was asserting that
what he was promising
regarding conception and childbirth
could not happen to her
as happens to other women.

When she had attentively heard
faithfully believed
and accepted with fitting desire
how it could be,
without any further hesitation
she answered:
Behold the handmaid of the Lord.
Be it done to me
according to your word[2]
according, that is,
to the way you have told me
and I have found pleasing.

Geoffrey of Auxerre[3]

[1] Lk 1:34
[2] Lk 1:38
[3] Sermon Fourteen on the Apocalypse

Behold,
she says,
I am the handmaiden of the Lord.
Be it unto me according to your word. [1]

Humility
is always found in company with divine grace,
for *God opposes the proud,*
but he gives grace to the humble. [2]

To prepare the throne of grace, therefore,
humility replied.
Behold,
she said,
I am the handmaid of the Lord.

What is this humility
so sublime
that it resists honor
and refuses to vaunt itself in glory?

She is chosen to be the mother of God,
and she calls herself a handmaid.

Surely, this is no insignificant sign of humility:
when glory is proposed
not to forget humility.

It is no great thing to be humble
when we are cast down,
but honored humility
is a great and rare virtue.

Bernard *of* Clairvaux [3]

[1] Lk 1:38
[2] Jas 4:6
[3] Homily Four in Praise of the Blessed Virgin Mary, 1

Mary conceived
by the Holy Spirit
not because
she received the seed of birth
from the substance of the Holy Spirit
but because
through the operation of the Holy Spirit
her nature ministered its substance
to the divine birth

Because love of the Holy Spirit
burned in her holy soul
in a singular way
the power of that same spirit
worked marvels in her flesh.

William *of* Saint Thierry [1]

---

[1] Exposition on the Epistle to the Romans 1.4

Hail Mary, full of grace
The Lord is with you. [1]

Every day we devoutly use this angelic salutation
just as it was given to us
to greet the most blessed Virgin.
But we normally add to it:
and blessed is the fruit of your womb. [2]

It was Elizabeth who added this closing passage,
for after she had been greeted by the Virgin,
she repeated, as it were,
the end of the angel's greeting
and went on to add:
Blessed are you among women
and blessed is the fruit of your womb.

This is the fruit of which Isaiah says:
In that day the shoot of the Lord
will be magnificent and glorious,
and the fruit of the earth will be high. [3]

What is this fruit
but holy Israel, which is also itself
the seed of Abraham,
the shoot of the Lord,
the flower which climbs from the root of Jesse,
the fruit of life in which we share.

Blessed indeed in the seed,
and blessed in the shoot,
blessed in the flower,
blessed in the gift, and
blessed, finally, in the giving of thanks
and in the proclamation [of praise].

Christ,
the seed of Abraham,
was descended from the seed of David
according to the flesh.[4]

Yet if the Virgin,
who was pledged to Joseph of the house of David,
was herself of the seed of David;
and if Christ was born of woman [5]
from whom he was born without seed
—of the seed of David,[6] that is,
without seed [7] —
why, then,
do we not devoutly believe that
Christ was wholly descended from the seed of David?

Without seed.
Why does it say this?
Because the Virgin was found to be with child
by the Holy Spirit,
because she conceived in a marvellous way
and from the normal processes of reproduction
she took nothing.

From herself
she provided the substance of the flesh [of Christ]
and in taking flesh from her
he remained undefiled.

Baldwin *of* Forde [8]

[1] Cf Lk 1:28
[2] Lk 1:42
[3] Is 4:2
[4] Rm 1:3
[5] Gal 4:4
[6] Jn 7:42

[7] From the antiphon *O admirabile commercium*, sung at Vespers on the Feast of the Purification, 2 February.
[8] Tractate 7

The angel Gabriel was sent by God
to a town of Galilee
called Nazareth.[1]

Do you wonder why Nazareth,
a small town,
should be made illustrious by the messenger of such
a king
and such a messenger?

A great treasure is hidden in this little town
hidden, I say, from human beings
not from God.

Is Mary not God's treasure?

Wherever she is,
there is his heart also.[2]

His eyes are on her.
Everywhere he looks upon the lowliness
of his handmaiden.[3]

Does the Only-begotten of God the Father
know heaven?
If he knows that,
he knows Nazareth too.

How would he not be familiar with his homeland?
How should he not know his heritage?

He claims heaven
from his Father
Nazareth
from his mother,
as he testifies that
he is both David's Son and Lord.[4]

The heaven of heavens belongs to the Lord
but the earth has he given to the children of men.[5]

Bernard *of* Clairvaux[6]

[1] Lk 1:26
[2] Cf. Mt 6:21
[3] Lk 1:48
[4] Mt 22:42-43
[5] Ps 115:16
[6] Sermon Three for the Feast
of the Annunciation, 7

The flowers have appeared on our earth.[1]

No one disputes that Nazareth means 'flower'.

The flower from the root of Jesse[2]
loves his flowery homeland,
and *the flower of the field* and *the lily of the valley*
feeds gladly *among the lilies.*[3]

Beauty, sweetness, and the hope of fruit
—a threefold gift—
commend flowers.

You also
God reckons a flower
and he is well pleased with you [4]
if you do not lack
the comeliness
of a decent way of life
the fragrance
of a good reputation
and the intention
of gaining a future reward.

The fruit of the Spirit
is eternal life.[5]

Bernard *of* Clairvaux [6]

[1] Sg 2:12
[2] Is 11:1
[3] Sg 2:1,16

[4] Mt 3:17
[5] Ga 5:22., Rm 6:23
[6] Sermon Three for the Feast
of the Annunciation, 7

She was prefigured in mystic wonders
heralded in the oracles of prophets.
She is prefigured by
the rod of priest[1]
which flowered without a root;
Gideon's fleece[2]
which was damp in the midst of a dry field;
the eastern gate in Ezekiel's vision
which was open to none.[3]

Isaiah in particular
promised that a rod was to arise
from the root of Jesse:
clearly the virgin birth.

It is written
that a great sign appeared in heaven[4]
which was known to have been promised
long before.

The Lord himself
he said
shall give you a sign:
Behold a virgin shall conceive.[5]

Bernard of Clairvaux [6]

[1] Num 17:8
[2] Jdg 6:36-38
[3] Ezk 44:1-3
[4] Rev 12:1
[5] Is 7:14
[6] Sermon for the Octave of
the Feast of the Assumption, 8

Solomon

because he had read God's promise
that he who had prevailed over woman
would in turn be prevailed over by her
and realized that this was only right
he exclaimed, greatly amazed,[1]
Who shall find a valiant woman?[2]

This is to say:
if the salvation of all of us,
the restitution of our innocence
and the victory over the enemy
hang upon the hand of a woman,[3]
it becomes very necessary indeed
that he foresee
that she be equal
to so great a task ✍

The price of this valiant woman
is not known to man[4] on earth,
but is found in the heights of heaven,[5]
and not even in the heavens[6] nearest the earth,
but in the very heaven of heavens.[7] ✍

Aaron's rod
—which blossomed without being watered[8]—
what did it portend
if not Mary
who conceived although she knew no man?

The even greater mystery of this great miracle
Isaiah taught us
when he said:
There shall come forth a shoot from the rod of Jesse,
and a blossom shall grow out of its root.[9]

The rod
symbolized the Virgin
and the blossom
the virgin birth.

But perhaps you prefer the interpretation
which makes Christ out to be the blossom
↳
If so, you should realize that this same rod of Aaron
not only blossomed
but also put forth leaves
and bore fruit,
and that Christ was symbolized
not only by the blossom and fruit
but by the leaves as well.

You realize that in the case of the rod of Moses,
Christ was figured by neither fruit nor blossom,
but by the rod itself.[10]
↳
In the witness brought forward by Isaiah, however,
take the blossom
to mean the Son
and the rod
his mother,
for as the rod blossomed without seed,
so the Virgin conceived without man. ↳

Gideon's fleece
—having been shorn from the flesh
without drawing blood—
was laid on the threshing floor
where dew dropped down
once on the wool alone
and then only on the ground around it. [11]

Could this symbolize anything
except that flesh
which was taken from the Virgin's flesh
without harm being done to her virginity?
When the heavens dropped down from above,[12]
the fullness of the divine nature
poured itself on her,[13]
from which fullness
we have all received,[14]
and without which
we are nothing but dry land.[15]

Gideon's action seems to fit quite nicely
with the prophet's words,
where he says:
May he come down like rain upon the fleece.[16]

This abundant rain[17]
which God had stored up for his inheritance
fell with hushed silence into the virgin womb,
penetrating her gently
without the din[18] of human intervention.

You see
what an extraordinary miracle is accomplished
in and through the Virgin!
A miracle
which so many other miracles anticipated,
so many oracles promised.

One and the same spirit[19]
moved the prophets
and although they used differing signs at different
times
they foretold and foresaw
the same event
in many and various ways,[20]
but not by a varying spirit.

What was shown
to Moses in the bush and fire
to Aaron in the rod and blossom
to Gideon in the fleece and dew
Solomon perceived clearly
in the valiant woman and her price,
Jeremiah prophesied even more clearly. . .
Isaiah was the most explicit of all
when he spoken about the Virgin and God.
And the Angel Gabriel by his greeting
made it known
to the Virgin herself.[21]

For she it is
of whom the Evangelist writes when he says,
*The angel Gabriel was send from God
to a virgin engaged to Joseph.*[22]

Bernard of Clairvaux[23]

[1] Jdth 15:1
[2] Pr 31:10
[3] Jdth 16:1
[4] Job 28:13
[5] Sir 1:3
[6] Sir 1:5
[7] Ps 19:6
[8] Num 17:8
[9] Is 11:1
[10] Cf Jn 3:14
[11] Jdg 6:37-40
[12] Ps 68:9
[13] Col 2:9
[14] Jn 1:16
[15] Wis 19:7
[16] Ps 72:6
[17] Ps 68:9
[18] Cf 1 Cor 13:1
[19] 1 Cor 14:32
[20] Heb 1:1
[21] Lk 1:28
[22] Lk 1:26-27
[23] Homilies in Praise of the Blessed Virgin Mary, 2.4-11

Just as Thomas
putting out his hand in doubt
to touch the Lord
was to become a stout witness
to his resurrection
so Joseph
in engaging himself to Mary
watched over her reputation
by his protection
and thus became the faithful witness
to her modesty.

Thomas' doubt
and Mary's engagement
fit beautifully together.

In both instances
we risk being trapped in the snare
of a similar mistake
over his faith
and her purity
and into thinking our suspicion justified ♫

I
—weak man that I am—
I find it easier to believe in the Son's resurrection
when I see Thomas doubtfully touching him
than when I see Cephas believing on simple hearsay.

Likewise,
I have more faith
in the mother's purity
when I know that her fiancé watched over
and witnessed it
than I would if the Virgin defended herself
solely by her own conscience.[1]

Tell me, I say,
who
—knowing her to be unwedded and yet pregnant—
would not suspect her of being a harlot
rather than a virgin?

And it would not do at all
for such a thing to be rumored about
the Mother of our Lord ♫

It was necessary therefore
for Mary to be engaged to Joseph:
by this
what was holy
was kept secret from dogs;

her virginity was attested to
by her fiancé
the Virgin was spared
all shame
and her reputation was preserved.

What could be wiser or more worthy
of divine Providence?

Bernard *of* Clairvaux[2]

[1] Cf 2 Cor 1:12
[2] Homily Two in Praise of the Blessed Virgin Mary, 12-13

Not without good reason
was holy Joseph[1] born of a barren mother.
Barrenness in Rachel
prefigured the virginity of our Joseph's mother.

Nor is it without significance that
'Rachel' means 'sheep'.[2]

Much more aptly
can our Joseph's mother be called a sheep,
for upon her fleece came down heavenly rain
just as the holy David says:
He shall come down like rain upon a fleece.[3]

Fleece
—as someone has said[4]—
although it belongs to the body
knows nothing of the body's passions;
so virginity,
although it is in the flesh,
knows nothing of the vices of the flesh.

He shall come down like rain upon a fleece.[5]
A fleece can retain the moisture which comes from
above
but it cannot feel the moisture of carnal pleasure.

So too
the virginity of blessed Mary
obtained the dew
which came from heaven
but could feel no carnal pleasure.

What moreover is more befitting the Lamb
than that its mother be a sheep?
Notice then how appropriately she is called a sheep,
who gave birth to the heavenly *Lamb*
who takes away the sins of the world,[6]
who was led like a sheep to the slaughter
and like a lamb in the hands of the shearer
made no sound and opened not his mouth.[7]

Aelred of Rievaulx[8]

[1] Joseph the patriarch, Gen 30:22-24
[2] Jerome, *The Interpretation of Hebrew Names* 9; CCSL 72:70, 25 *et passim*
[3] Ps 71 [72]:6
[4] Pseudo-Jerome, *Letter* 9:5, in fact, Paschasius Radbertus, *De Assumptione S. Mariae Virginis,* 5:28 (CCSL 56c:121, 229-231)
[5] Ps 71 [72]:6
[6] Jn 1:29
[7] Is 53:7, Ac 8:32
[8] Sermon 9:12-13: On the Feast of the Annunciation

A fleece,
although it comes from the flesh,
grows outside the flesh
and knows not the sufferings of the flesh.

By its softness,
by its homely color,
it proclaims its gentleness and humility

By being easy to handle
it bears the mark of simplicity and innocence
and with its natural covering
it keeps warm
delicate limbs.

It betoken the glorious Virgin
who, dwelling in the flesh,
raised herself beyond the flesh
and slew the passions of the flesh
by the power of the Spirit.

For she is known to have lived
like no other
in gentleness and humility.

No one
will be able
adequately to describe
her simplicity and innocence.

The understanding does not grasp
the charity
by which she protects and unceasingly cherishes
the human race.

It remains to discuss
how the rain descends upon the fleece
and how the drops flow out over the earth.

The rain descends upon the fleece
without sound,
without movement,
without any cleavage
or division.

It is gently poured out
peacefully received
sweetly drunk.

Thus, the drops
gradually
little by little
spread over the earth,
falling down so wonderfully and so gently
that their coming is scarcely perceived
and as they depart
they bring forth the shoots.

In the same way
the rain coming from beyond,
above the heavenly waters,
came down into the Virgin's womb
without human act,
with no movement of concupiscence,
her integrity unimpaired
her virgin's doors still locked.

Gently was it poured
calmly received
ineffably made flesh.

It came
drop by drop
upon her soil,
unseen as it entered,
as it departed
plainly going forth.

Amadeus *of* Lausanne[1]

[1] Homily Three on the Praises of Blessed Mary

Consider a special sign of faith:
the Mother of the Lord.

Once she had received the good news
of our salvation
and of her conceiving
by the seal of the Holy Spirit
she believed
with absolute certainty
that she would be the Mother of the Lord.

Yet there was something
she wanted to know:
the manner
of fulfilling this mystery.

She asked:
How shall this be
for I do not know a man. [1]

The reality
she held by faith
but she wanted to know
the manner.

Her faithful soul
embraced the reality
—comforted by the very grace
of which she was full—
but her astonished nature
was wondering at the manner
by which it would happen.

Already
within herself
she was feeling
the Holy Spirit
operating in a unique way
but she did not know
how he would accomplish
in her flesh
without the help of flesh
the wonderful things she believed.

William *of* Saint Thierry[2]

[1] Lk 1:34
[2] The Mirror of Faith, 19

This is the singular glory of our Virgin
and Mary's surpassing privilege:
that in common with God the Father
she was worthy to have
one and the same Son.

This surely she would have missed
had the Son not been made flesh.
Yet no other like opportunity could be given us
for the inheritance and the salvation
so much hoped for.

Bernard *of* Clairvaux [1]

[1] Second Sermon for the Feast of the Annunciation, 2

Today
the Word was made flesh
and began to dwell *among us.*[1]

Today
Wisdom began to build for himself
the house of our body
in the Virgin's womb.

And for the building up of the Church's unity
he hewed out the cornerstones[2]
from the mountain
without the labor of hands.[3]

Without the intervention of man
he fashioned for himself
from a virginal body
the flesh of our redemption.

From this day forward
the Lord of hosts is with us.

Guerric of Igny [4]

[1] Jn 1:14
[2] Cf Eph 2:20
[3] Dan 3:24
[4] Sermon 27.1: Second Sermon for the Feast of the Annunciation

Blessed are You Among Women

In those days Mary arose and went with haste into the hill country, to a city of Judah, and she entered the house of Zechariah and greeted Elizabeth. And when Elizabeth heard the greeting of Mary, the babe leaped in her womb; and Elizabeth was filled with the Holy Spirit and she exclaimed with a loud cry, 'Blessed are you among women, and blessed is the fruit of your womb! And why is this granted me, that the mother of my Lord should come to me? For behold, when the voice of your greeting came to my ears, the babe in my womb leaped for joy. And blessed is she who believed that there would be a fulfilment of what was spoken to her from the Lord.'

And Mary said, 'My soul magnifies the Lord, and my spirit rejoices in God my Saviour, for he has regarded the low estate of his handmaiden. For behold, henceforth all generations will call me blessed; for he who is mighty has done great things for me, and holy is his name. And his mercy is on those who fear him from generation to generation. He has shown strength with his arm, he has scattered the proud in the imagination of their hearts, he has put down the mighty from their thrones, and exalted those of low degree; he has filled the hungry with good things, and the rich he has sent empty away. He has helped his servant Israel, in remembrance of his mercy, as he spoke to our fathers, to Abraham and to his posterity for ever.'

And Mary remained with her about three months, and returned to her home.

Luke 1: 39-56

Listen now to the Evangelist:
Rising up,
he says,
Mary set out in haste for the hill country,
to the home of Zachary
and greeted Elizabeth.[1]

Let us add this, too:
Joseph also went up to Bethlehem
together with Mary, his betrothed wife, who was with child.[2]

Reflect
in all this
on her wonderful humility.

She,
filled with God
greater than the world
higher than heaven
more fertile than Paradise
the splendor of virgins
the glory of women
the praise of humankind
the gladness of angels
she whom the Son of God chose
to be his mother,
called herself a handmaiden.

She
whom the angel greeted
subjected herself in great obedience to a workman.

She,
the queen of heaven
the mistress of the angels
who bore God in her womb,
greeted her kinswoman humbly
because she was older than herself.

How very right it is then to say of blessed Mary:
You are beautiful and fair,
utterly chaste in the midst of delights.[3]

If we can appraise this beauty well
we shall see that what was said of Rachel
applies to no one more aptly than to
the mother of our Joseph:

She had a beautiful face and a charming appearance.[4]

Aelred *of* Rievaulx [5]

[1] Lk 1:39-40
[2] Lk 2:4-5
[3] Sg 7:6
[4] Gen 29:17; 39:6
[5] Sermon 9.24-25: On the Feast
of the Annunciation

Ascending into the hill country
she greeted Elizabeth.

At her voice,
John
—enclosed in the womb—
rejoiced with a novel joy.[1]

And although she could have been carried away
with the great news
she burst out in a song
of thanksgiving and praise[2]
magnifying the Lord[3]
and rendering thanks to him
as the source of all benefits.

Geoffrey *of* Auxerre [4]

[1] Cf. Lk 1:42, 44
[2] Cf Ps 42: Ps 42:4, Jon 2:9
[3] Lk 1:46
[4] Sermon 14 on the Apocalypse

When Mary came up to Elizabeth
the unique glory of the Virgin
was immediately revealed to her
by the Spirit.

Then she marveled at the person who had come,
saying
How does it happen to me
that the mother of my Lord should come to me?[1]

And she extolled the voice of the one greeting her,
adding:
When the voice of your greeting sounded in my ears
the child leapt in my womb for joy;[2]
and she blessed the faith of her who believed,
saying
Blessed are you who believed
for the things which were spoken to you by the Lord
shall be done in you.[3]

A powerful declaration!
Yet her devout humility let her keep nothing for
herself
instead she poured it all back on him
whose goodness to her she praised.

She said:
you magnify the mother of the Lord
but *my soul magnifies the Lord.*

At my voice
you claim that your son leapt for joy
but *my spirit has rejoiced in God my Saviour.*
And he,
like the bridegroom's friend
rejoices at the voice of his beloved.

Bernard *of* Clairvaux [4]

[1] Lk 2:24
[2] Lk 1:44
[3] Lk 1:45
[4] Sermon for the Octave of the Assumption, 12

As Mary's voice
sounds in Elizabeth's ears
it penetrates to John's heart
—there where he lies hidden within his mother's
womb—
it gives life to his spirit
and feeds him with salutary joy.

Although the power of nature
had as yet scarcely finished imparting his soul[1]
the power of Mary's voice imparts
the gift of prophecy in all its fullness
so that it seems to be communicated abundantly
from the son's fullness
to the mother.

In truth,
Mary was full of grace.[2]

The God of all grace
was clearly in her
when from his liberality
grace's generous gift flowered
both abundantly and magnificently
in the first place into this mother
from his mother into John,
from John into his parents.

Rivers of living water
flowed from Mary's bosom. [3]
A fountain of life and grace
rose from the midst of Paradise
to water the trees of paradise.[4]

Guerric of Igny [5]

[1] In the Middle Ages it was believed that the soul was infused into a male child forty days after physical conception, and eighty days after a girl's conception.
[2] Lk 1:28
[3] Cf. Jn 7:38
[4] Cf Gen 2:6,10.
[5] Sermon 40.2, First Sermon for the Feast of the Nativity of John the Baptist, 24 June.

When blessed Elizabeth
was filled with the Holy Spirit,[1]
as we have heard,
she recognized a greater grace
in the Virgin
and was amazed
that she visited and greeted her.

How is it, she said,
that the mother of my Lord should come to me?[2]

Since she had been greeted herself,
she was right to greet her
through whom salvation had to be imparted,
for in this way
she rendered thanks to God,
who gives salvation to kings [3]
and who commands the saving of Jacob. [4]

Mary was indeed full of grace
in good measure
pressed down
shaken together
and running over [5]
and for this reason:
that through her
the grace of God might abound
in us.

God chose her
in advance
in a unique way
and accorded her the grace of being endowed
with a triple grace:
the grace of beauty
the grace of favor
and the grace of honor
so that she should be made
beautiful
gracious
and glorious.

Baldwin of Forde[6]

[1] Lk 1:41
[2] Lk 1:43
[3] Ps 143 (144):10
[4] Ps 43:5 (44:4)
[5] Lk 6:38
[6] Tractate 7

Let us listen to Jeremiah prophesying 🖉
The Lord has created a new thing on earth
a woman shall enclose a man. [1] 🖉

If I direct my attention to
this virginal conception
I shall discover
—among the many new and marvelous things
to be seen
by someone who searches diligently [2] —
this very novelty
which I cited from the prophet.

In it one recognizes
short length [3]
narrow breadth [4]
lowly height
level depth.

There one perceives
an unshining light
a speechless word
parched water
famished bread.

If you look carefully you will see
sad joy
timorous trust
ailing health
inanimate life
frail strength.

But
–which is just as amazing–
you will also see
sadness giving joy
fear giving comfort
pain healing
death vivifying
weakness fortifying.

Surely, then, I shall also discover
that very marvel for which I am looking.

Surely among all these [paradoxes]
when you see Mary
bearing in her womb
Jesus
the man approved by God
you cannot fail to recognize
the woman enclosing a man.

Bernard *of* Clairvaux [5]

[1] Jer 31:22
[2] Cf Mt 2:7-8
[3] Cf Eph 3:8
[4] Cf Rom 8:39
[5] Homily Two in Praise of the Blessed Virgin Mary, 9

She who humbled herself
—we believe—
so much more than any other
that she was to that extent more worthy;

she who alone says,
My soul magnifies the Lord,
she magnified him more
who had herself been more magnified
and raised up to such eminence
that she alone can say,
He who is mighty has done great things for me.[1]

And having been magnified more,
she magnified God more
because she humbled herself more
and bore witness herself
to her own humility,
saying humbly,
He has regarded the humility of his handmaid.[2]

Elizabeth too was a witness,
for when the Mother of God visited her
she extolled equally her happiness,
her dignity,
and, in that great dignity,
her humility.

For great humility in great dignity
is always admirable,
and so too is great humility in great power,
or great humility
in wisdom,
eloquence
or virtue.

In a word,
in anything great,
great humility
is the balancing feature.

It arranges and orders the face
and conforms and regulates everything
so that all the various parts
are in harmony.

Baldwin *of* Forde [3]

[1] Lk 1:49
[2] Lk 1:48
[3] Tractate 7

She is loved
and praised
and honored by all.

For men and for angels,
she
after God,
is the first [object of]
love
and praise
and honor.

The whole church of the saints proclaims her praises:
The daughters of Sion saw her and declared her most blessed;
the queens and concubines praised her. [1]

Nor does she herself pass over in silence
this grace of such great favor:

All generations, she says,
will call me blessed. [2]

Baldwin of Forde [3]

[1] Sg 6:8
[2] Lk 1:48
[3] Tractate 7

She Gave Birth
to her First-born Son

And Joseph also went up from Galilee, from the city of Nazareth, to Judea, to the city of David, which is called Bethlehem, because he was of the house and lineage of David, to be enrolled with Mary, his betrothed, who was with child. And while they were there, the time came for her to be delivered. And she gave birth to her first-born son and wrapped him in swaddling cloths, and laid him in a manger, because there was no place for them in the inn.

Luke 2:6-7

Virgin and mother.
Astounding and unique.

Never
since the world began
has it been heard[1]
that a virgin has given birth,
that a mother has remained a virgin.

Never
in the ordinary course of events
is there virginity
where fruitfulness is mentioned
nor fruitfulness
where virginity is maintained with integrity.

She is the only person
in whom virginity and fruitfulness have met.[2]

Here
—just once—
something happened
which never happened before
and never will again.

Bernard *of* Clairvaux [3]

[1] Jn 9:32
[2] Ps 85.10

[3] Third Sermon for
Christmas, 9

Christic came forth

His coming forth is from the days of eternity.[1]
But at the end of the ages
his coming forth
is from the womb of the woman
who encompassed him.

If the Lord wrought something
new upon earth
still the fragrance of this wonderful news
filled the heavens.

A woman will encompass a man
as a crown encompasses the head.

For the *head of the Church is Christ.*[2]

Gilbert *of* Hoyland [3]

---

[1] Micah 5:2
[2] Eph 5:23
[3] Sermon 21 on the Song of Songs, 2

When Jesus left his mother's body
in which he had been cherished and nourished
he left behind him
a blessing.

He sanctified her womb
when he entered it;
he filled it
when he dwelt within it;
and then, when he bade it farewell
he consecrated it
and strengthened it
with his full blessing.

That blessing overflowed on outward things
but without losing its first grace
which it continually poured into her.

Jesus came forth from his mother
so as to bless her virginal eyes as well
by showing her his face.

He came forth
to sanctify her mouth
with the beautiful kiss of his own mouth[1]
to make blessed her breasts
by pressing his lips to them
to consecrate her hands
her lap
her knees
every part of her
by the infinite sweetness of his sacred body
as she held him to her.

John *of* Ford [2]

The Virgin Bearer of God is the bough[1]
her Son the blossom.

The Son of the Virgin
the blossom
a blossom white and ruddy,
chosen out of thousands,
a blossom on which the angels long to gaze
a blossom at whose scent the dead are raised to life.
A blossom of the field
—as he himself bears witnesses—
not of the garden.

The field blossoms
without human help
not sown by anyone
not cultivated by a spade
not fertilized with dung.

Thus did the Virgin's womb blossom
inviolate, intact, chaste
as from an eternally verdant pasture
bringing forth a Blossom
whose beauty will never see corruption
whose glory will not ever fade.

 Bernard *of* Clairvaux [2]

---

[1] A play on the words Virgin and bough: *Virgo-virga*.
[2] Second Sermon for Advent, 2

No human being
has any inkling of the grace
that suffused her loving gaze.

It was
the gaze of one who contemplated
eye to eye
that great mystery of tender love
a gaze that beheld
face to face
that great brilliancy of light.

Even if the human weakness of the child she bore
and her constant knowledge of his baby needs
may sometimes have cast a cloud
over her contemplation
of his glorious face,
from the cloud[1]
the Holy Spirit overshadowed her
and from the cloud
the Father of the Lord Jesus
thundered the words
This is my beloved Son[2]
and he is your beloved son, too.

John *of* Ford [3]

[1] Cf Lk 1:35
[2] Mt 3:17
[3] Sermon 75 on the Song of Songs, 3

An angel
announces to Mary
the Lord's conception.
An angel
announces his birth
to the shepherds.

Indeed not only to the shepherds
but to the angels themselves
an angel
seems to have made the announcement.

One proclaims
while the others applaud.

There was with the angel
says Luke
a multitude of the heavenly host
praising God and singing
Glory to God in the highest.[1]

One announces
what the others knew equally well
and yet they hear
as something new and recent
what could not be unknown to them.

O blessed is this wonderful news
which affords joy
to the hearing of angels,
which makes them delight
in listening
and–as it were–
learning again from another
what truth itself taught them
from the beginning.

Gilbert *of* Hoyland [2]

[1] Lk 2:8-14
[2] Sermon 21 on the Song of Songs, 1

Let us weigh carefully
the difference
between the child-bearing
of Mary
and
of Eve.

Eve bore a child, being corrupt.
Mary brought forth, being incorrupt.
Eve in pain,
Mary in health.
Eve in the 'old man'
Mary in the new.
Eve brought forth a slave,
Mary a Lord.
Eve a guilty one,
Mary a righteous one.
Eve a sinner,
Mary One who justifies from sin.

The child-bearing of Eve multiplies deaths,
that of Mary saves from death.
While Eve gives birth, the dragon lies in wait.
At Mary's child-bearing angels minister.

Terror of heart seizes upon Eve in labor,
as Mary brings forth, divine power gladdens her.

Those, Eve, whom you brought forth
you expose to many misfortunes.
Your offspring, Mary,
you save from all evil.
As Eve gave birth, malice abounded,
but when Mary did, grace superabounded.

At Mary's child-bearing,
the good rejoiced
and the wicked were dismayed
for he was being born
who would render good things to the good
and strike the evil with the vengeance they deserved.

Consider
that when the mother gave birth
the face of the universe smiled
and the glad world applauded its Lord.

Reflect
that the clouds were swept away
and the sky put on its beauty
and the stars, saying *here we are*[1]
blazed with joy
for him.

Reflect
that night poured forth light in the darkness
and instead of blackness offered radiance
that night gave light before the sun arose
and a brightness
which from its exceeding brilliance
obscured the splendor of the sun.

Of this night,
the psalmist says:
Night is my light in my delights [2]
and, turning to the Lord he follows and says,
The darkness will not be dark with you
and the night will be as bright as the day [3]
for God's darkness is as his light.

If all things rejoiced at his birth,
how did his mother rejoice?
If all things were glad,
how great a gladness did she enjoy?
If all things were so glad
what happiness was in the mother?

At the weight of a joy so great
the tongue falters
the heart fails
the mind is aghast.

How could so frail a vessel
—still made of clay and mortal—
hold out before such mighty joys?

For at the birth of Christ
he overshadowed her
who overshadowed her at his conception.

He gave her the power
to bear the joys,
he who granted her the wealth
and the strength of his divinity
with wondrous power controlled her
whom the glory of his majesty
filled with unspeakable richness.

When she had brought forth
the promised Son
and had given birth
to the day from day
for our day,
turning to God with her whole heart
she gave voice to her thanks and praise on high,
offered the acceptable sacrifice of her lips
and offered the sacrifice of her jubilation,[4]
gave the peaceful holocaust of her heart
and for a burnt offering to the Lord
sacrificed the sweet perfumed incense.[5]

Taking up the new-born Emmanuel
she beheld a light incomparably fairer than the sun
and saw a fire that water cannot quench.

She received in the covering of the flesh
`she had borne
the light that lightens all things
and she was worthy to carry in her arms
the Word
that carries the universe.

She marvels that she, a virgin,
has become a mother
and with joy marvels
that she is the Mother of God.

She knows that in her have been fulfilled
the promise of the patriarchs,
the oracles of the prophets
and the longings of the fathers of old,
who foretold that Christ would be born of a virgin
and with all their prayers awaited his birth.

Amadeus *of* Lausanne [6]

[1] Bar 3:35
[2] Ps 138:11
[3] Ps 139:12
[4] Cf. Ps 27:6

[5] Cf. Dt 27:7, Lev 4:31
[6] Homily 4 on the Praises of
Blessed Mary

What are we to make
of the Lord's declaration to Ezechiel:
*This door shall be closed
it shall not be opened?*[1]

What shall be opened to the Lord
is not the integrity of the Virgin's body
—for, as Ezechiel added:
This shall be closed even to the prince himself—
but the ear
and the door of the heart.

For it was through the Virgin's ear
that the Word entered to become incarnate
and through the closed door of her body
that he came forth incarnate.

Guerric of Igny [2]

[1] Ezek 44:2
[2] Second Sermon for the Feast of the Annunciation, 2

For this cause
was the Word made flesh,
that
by the flesh
it might draw the flesh

and that joining flesh to flesh
by the bond of charity
It might bring back the wandering sheep
to the invisible things of God
and to the invisible omnipotent Father.[1]

Because, deserting God,
that sheep
fell in the flesh.
It needed by the mystery of this incarnate hand
to be lifted up
and returned to the Father
as in a sort of carriage.

With this midwife hand, therefore,
Mary not only felt no pain
but remained virgin
even in giving birth.

She is the door
concerning which we read in the book of Ezeckiel:
that door will remain closed for the prince
and through it the prince will go forth.[2]

Through this door
Christ, prince of the kings of the earth,[3]
has indeed issued
and just as in entering
He did not open it,
so in leaving
He did not unclose it.

He passed through in peace,
and his path was not seen.

But if you marvel
that God was born
while Mary's womb remained closed
and sealed with her virgin purity,

marvel also
that though the door of the sepulchre
was closed and sealed,
he returned
to the upper world

and when the doors were locked
came in to his disciples.[4]

For we are not removing your wonder,
but keeping at bay your unbelief.

Whatsoever he willed,
the Lord did,[5]

and all his works may be wondered at,
but not examined.

Amadeus of Lausanne[6]

[1] Cf. Lk 15:5-6
[2] Ezk 44:2-3
[3] Rev 1:5
[4] Jn 20:19
[5] Ps 135:6
[6] Homily 4 on the Praises of
Blessed Mary

God

—for it was indeed God whom she bore—
having it in mind to give his mother special glory in
heaven,
was careful to prepare her on earth
with a special grace
whereby she conceived
undefiled beyond all telling
and unspoiled,
she gave birth.

Only this mode of birth was becoming to God
—to be born of a virgin.
The only childbearing becoming to a virgin
is to give birth to God alone.[1]

So it was that the Maker of humankind[2]
in order to become human,
born of human flesh,
out of all the living had to choose[3]
one person,
or rather,
he had to create someone
whom he knew would be worthy[4]
to be his mother,
someone in whom he was sure he could delight.

That was why he wanted her to be a virgin,
someone unstained
from whom he himself could be born stainless,
for he was to wipe away all our stains.[5]

He wanted her to be humble as well,
someone of whom he could himself be born
gentle and humble of heart,[6]
because he intended to give all humankind
the necessary and most beneficial example of these
virtues.

So he gave the blessing of childbirth
to the virgin
in whom he had first inspired the vow of virginity
and from who he had first demanded humility.

Had it been otherwise,
that is, had there been in her any good
–however slight–
which was not a gift of grace,
how could the angel have proclaimed her
in the terms he does:
full of grace?[7]
That she might conceive and give birth
to the Holy of Holies[8]
she was made holy in her body
by the gift of virginity
and she accepted that gift of humility
to become holy in spirit too.

And this is what the Evangelist is telling us here
when he states that
an angel was sent from God to a virgin:[9]
from the Highest
to the humble;
from the Master
to the maiden;
from the Creator
to the creature.
How kind God is!
How matchless is the virgin!

Bernard *of* Clairvaux [10]

[1] Ps 62:1
[2] Is 17:7
[3] Sir 45:16
[4] Wis 6:16
[5] Jn 1:29
[6] Mt 11:29
[7] Lk 1:28
[8] Dan 9:24
[9] Lk 1:26-27
[10] Homily Two in Praise of the Blessed Virgin Mary, 1-2

This fruitful virginity
is indeed a wonderful new thing,
yet far more wonderful
is the novelty of the Child born of it.

No one
who admits
that the Child was God
finds any difficulty in believing
his mother remained a virgin.

His birth
could in no way injure
the physical integrity of his
even the diseased whole.

Nor could the reality of the body he assumed
be thought to limit the power of the Creator
as if he could not retain for himself
what he gives to many of his creatures.

For you find not a few creatures
that are born without any harm
to the integrity of the parents.

In their own way
they all bear witness
to the Creator's own immaculate birth.

But the mother herself
—quite aware of the mystery surrounding her—
has spoken and taught us
how and what she brought forth.

She speaks, however
not in contemporary or recent arguments
but in the ancient oracles of prophecy
because, as the apostle Peter tells us:
the word of prophecy
is a stronger witness than miracles [1] ⧸⟞

Long before her birth
the Spirit
who would later make his dwelling in her
borrowed Mary's voice
to defend against the blasphemies of unbelievers
both the divinity of the Child
and the integrity of the mother
—all his own handiwork.

In her person
—if we are to follow a common opinion—
he uttered the words you have just heard:
As the vine
I have brought forth a pleasant odor.[2]

In their context
these words must be applied
to the person of Wisdom himself,
that is,
the Son.

But you know quite well
from the rules of Holy Scripture[3]
that this does not mean that these
—like so many other—passages
cannot be applied as well
to the mother,

Let Mary reply ⨏
Let her put an end to all heresies
with a single word:
As a vine
I have brought forth a pleasant odor.

It is as if she were saying:
'My childbearing is unique among womankind
but it has its like among things of nature.
Do you want to know
how virginity gave birth to the Saviour?
In the same way
as the flower of the vine produces its fragrance.
If ever you find the flower corrupted
by giving off its sweet odor,
then you may hold that my virginity was violated
in giving birth to my Saviour.'

Can you find fault with the simile?
What else is virginity
than the flower of an undefiled body?
What else is the Child of virginity
than its sweet odor?

 Guerric of Igny [4]

[1] Cf. 2 Peter 1:19
[2] Sir 24:23, read at Vespers and at Mass on the Feast of the Nativity of Mary.
[3] Reading Scripture at four levels: historically (literally), allegorically, anagogically, tropologically (morally).
[4] Sermon 51.3: On the Feast of the Nativity of Mary

She glories in childbirth
not, as I have said, for itself
but in him
whom she has borne:
God.
For it was indeed God
whom she bore
who had it in mind
to give his mother special glory in heaven
and was careful to prepare her on earth
with a special grace
whereby she conceived undefiled beyond all telling
and unspoiled she gave birth.

Only this mode of birth
was becoming to God:
to be born of a virgin.

The only childbearing becoming to a virgin
is to give birth to God alone.

So it was that
the Maker of humankind[1]
in order to become man
born of human flesh
had to choose one person out of all the living
or rather
he had to create someone
who he knew would be worthy to be his mother
someone in whom he was sure he could delight.[2]

That was why he wanted her to be a virgin
someone unstained
from whom he himself could be born stainless
for he was to wipe away all our stains.

He wanted her also to be
humble
someone of whom he could himself be born
gentle and humble of heart
because he intended to give
all humankind
the necessary and most beneficial example
of these virtues.

So he now gave the blessing of childbirth
to the virgin
in whom he had first inspired
the vow of virginity
and from whom
he had first demanded humility.

Had it been otherwise,
that is
had there been in her any good
however slight
which was not a gift of grace
how could the angel have proclaimed her
full of grace?

Bernard *of* Clairvaux [3]

[1] Is 17:7
[2] Mal 3:1
[3] Homily Two in Praise of the Blessed Virgin Mary, 1

Blessed Mary!
She lacks neither humility nor virginity.
And what unique virginity!
Motherhood did not stain,
but honored it.

What extraordinary humility!
Fruitful virginity did not tarnish,
but exalted it.
And matchless fruitfulness went hand in hand
with both virginity and humility.

Which of them is not wonderful?
Which is not incomparable?
Which is not unique?

I should not be at all surprised if
—having meditated upon them—
you hesitated to say which you find more praiseworthy:
whether you think more amazing
the fruitfulness in the virgin
or
the integrity in the mother;
nobility in child-bearing
or
—in spite of such nobility—
humility.

Possibly it is more excellent to have all three together
than to have one of them alone.
For there is no doubt that she, who was thus
thrice blessed,
was more blessed than if she had received
only one of them.

And yet is it so extraordinary that God
—whom we read and see to be wonderful in his
saints[1]—
should show himself even more wonderful
in his mother?

You who are married, then,
reverence the integrity of her flesh amid frail flesh.

And you consecrated virgins,
admire the virgin's fruitfulness.

Let everyone strive to imitate the humility
of the Mother of God.

Holy angels,
revere the mother of your King!

You angels
who worship our humble virgin's Child
—for he is your King and ours
the restorer of our race
the builder of your city—
allow us human beings to join with you
in singing worthy praise
of his highness
and his lowliness,
he who with you is
so sublime
and yet with us
so humble.

To him be honor and glory
for evermore.
Amen.

Bernard *of* Clairvaux [2]

[1] Ps 68:35
[2] Homily One in Praise of the Blessed Virgin Mary, 9

We believe
that the virgin conceived
and bore a Son.

We have
as an assuring sign
both the Mother and the Son.

For us the Mother is wholly a miracle
she who extraordinarily
and unprecedentedly
is mother and virgin.

For us the Son is wholly a miracle
who not only extraordinarily
but also incomprehensibly
is God and man.

The Virgin mother
conceiving and giving birth
is for us a sign
that he who is conceived and brought forth
is God and man.

The Son doing the things of God
and suffering the things of man
is for us a sign
that he raises up to God
man
for whom he is conceived and brought forth
and for whom also he suffers.

Guerric of Igny [1]

[1] Sermon 27:4: Sermon Three for the Feast of the Annunciation

Whatever the human tongue can say
is it not less than
what the Virgin Mary deserves?

If we truly appreciate the dignity of the woman
whom we are attempting to praise
whatever our human weakness can proclaim
in her honor
is meager and insufficient.

How could a human being
a sinner
do justice in praising the woman
by whom the Creator of humankind and of angels
chose to be born?

This is the mother of God
the queen of heaven
the pledge of our hope
whom we are endeavoring to praise.

What we have begun is not in our power
it is beyond us ♫

The Word of God
sanctified this tabernacle
and entered it once it was made holy.

Going forth from it
he preserved it in holiness.

It is written:
He is my God;
his way is pure.[1]

♫ Bernard *of* Clairvaux [2]

[1] Ps 18:30
[2] Sentences 3.111

Who shall declare this *generation?*[1]

An angel announces
the power of the Most High overshadows
the Spirit comes.[2]

The Virgin believes.
By faith the Virgin conceives.
The Virgin gives birth;
she remains a virgin.
Who would not marvel?

The Son of the Most High
is born:
God begotten of God before all ages.
The Word is born,
an infant.

Who can marvel enough at this?

Bernard *of* Clairvaux [3]

[1] Is 53:8 (Vulgate)
[2] Lk 1:35
[3] Sermon for Christmas Eve

The Purification of Mary

When the time came for their purification according to the law of Moses, they brought him up to Jerusalem to present him to the Lord (as it is written in the law of the Lord, 'Every male that opens the womb shall be called holy to the Lord') and to offer a sacrifice according to what is said in the law of the Lord, 'a pair of turtledoves, or two young pigeons.'

Now there was a man in Jerusalem, whose name was Simeon, and this man was righteous and devout, looking for the consolation of Israel, and the Holy Spirit was upon him. And it had been revealed to him by the Holy Spirit that he should not see death before he had seen the Lord's Christ. And inspired by the Spirit he came into the temple; and when the parents brought in the child Jesus, to do for him according to the custom of the law, he took him up in his arms and blessed God and said, 'Lord, now let your servant depart in peace, according to your word. For my eyes have seen your salvation, which thou hast prepared in the presence of all peoples, a light for revelation to the Gentiles, and for glory to thy people Israel.'

And his father and his mother marveled at what was said about him; and Simeon blessed them and said to Mary his mother, 'Behold, this child is set for the fall and rising of many in Israel, and for a sign that is spoken against that the thoughts of many hearts may be revealed—and a sword will pierce through your own soul also.'

And there was a prophetess, Anna, the daughter of Phanuel, of the tribe of Asher; she was of a great age, having lived with her husband seven years from her virginity, and as a widow till she was eighty_four. She did not depart from the temple, worshiping with fasting and prayer night and day. And coming up at that very hour she gave thanks to God, and spoke of him to all who were looking for the redemption of Jerusalem.

And when they had performed everything according to the law of the Lord, they returned into Galilee, to their own city, Nazareth. And the child grew and became strong, filled with wisdom; and the favor of God was upon him.

Luke 2:22-40

When the time had come
for Mary's purification.[1]

When Scripture relates the mysteries
of our redemption
it describes the historical events
which were enacted for us
in such a way as to indicate
what moral line of action we have to take.

As today we recall the purification of Blessed Mary,
we are clearly admonished
as to our own purification.
Who will not be moved
by the authority of such an example?

We see her
—the most holy of holy women—
although she had nothing to purify
consenting none the less
to fulfill the commandment of legal purification.

O immaculate Mother
O Mother untouched,
are you not aware of your own purity,
aware, that is, that
neither conception nor childbirth violated
but consecrated
your integrity?

Why then
—as if you had suffered
something of what is the common lot of woman
in conceiving or giving birth—
do you seek the remedies of a cleansing
which was provided for woman's weakness?

'It is right'
she says,
'that we should thus fulfill all justice,
so that I
who have been chosen
as the mother of supreme justice
should be also a mirror and a pattern of all justice ...

'The mother of prevarication sinned
and stubbornly defended herself.

The mother of redemption will not sin
and will make humble satisfaction
so that the offspring of humankind
who derive the impulse to sin
from the mother of all that is old
may obtain at least humility
from the mother of all that is new.'

Guerric of Igny [2] [1]

[1] Lk 2:22
[2] Sermon 18.1: Fourth Sermon for the Feast of the Purification

In the Law[1]
it was written
that a woman who
—having received seed—
has borne a son
should be unclean for seven days.
And on the eighth day she should circumcise the boy.

Then, while she was intent on
cleansing and purification,
she was to refrain from entering the temple for
thirty-three days.
After that time she was to offer her son to the Lord,
along with gifts.[2]

Does anyone fail to notice
that the Lord's mother is set free from this precept
at the very first phrase of this judgement?

Do you suppose
that when Moses was about to say that a woman
who has borne a son is unclean
he was not afraid of incurring the sin of blasphemy
against the Lord's mother,
and hence set down at the beginning,
having received a seed

This shows clearly that this law does not apply
to the Lord's mother.
Without having received seed
she gave birth to a son
just as Jeremiah had foretold.

The Lord chose to do a new thing on the earth.
Do you ask what this new thing is?
A woman, he says, *will encompass a man.*[3]
She will not receive a man by another man.
She will not conceive a human being
in the human way;
but in a womb untouched and blameless
she will enclose a man.

This was so that,
while the Lord was coming and going,
the eastern gate
—as another prophet says—
might remain permanently shut. [4]

Do you suppose
that her mind could not have been moved to say,
'What need have I of purification?
Why should I refrain from entering the temple?
My womb, not knowing man,
has become the temple of the Holy Spirit.

Why should I,
who have given birth to the Lord of the temple
not enter the temple?

Nothing in this conception and this birth
has been impure,
nothing unlawful,
nothing requiring purification.

This child I have brought forth
is the source of purification
and comes to make purification for transgressions:[5]
what can observation of the law purify in me?
I have been made absolutely pure
by the spotless birth itself.'

Truly blessed Virgin,
you have no reason for purification,
nor any need of it.

But —
had your child any need of circumcision?
Be among women as one of the their number,
just as your son was among the boys.

He willed to be circumcised.
Does he not will far more to be offered [to God]?

Offer your son,
holy Virgin,
and hold up to the Lord
the blessed fruit of your womb.[6]

Offer a sacrifice
holy and acceptable to God,[7]
for the reconciliation of us all.

God the Father will accept
the new oblation,
the most precious sacrifice,
of whom he himself said,
This is my beloved Son in whom I am well pleased.[8]

Bernard *of* Clairvaux[9]

[1] Lev 12:2-4
[2] Lev 12:6-8
[3] Jer 31:22
[4] 2 Ch 23:7; Ezk 44:2
[5] Heb 1:3

[6] Lk 1:42
[7] Rom 12:1
[8] Mt 17:5
[9] Sermon for the Feast of the Purification, 3

Mary was not purified.
Rather she put before us
the inner meaning
of purification.

In fulfilling the legal rite
she gave it a spiritual meaning.

For what could be purified in her
who had
conceived as a virgin,
given birth as a virgin
and remained still a virgin?

If beforehand her purity lacked anything at all,
she was fully purified
in this conceiving.

What was there to be purified
in that conception,
the one source of cleansing
for those who are conceived unclean?

He it is
who is revealed today,
he
who gives rise to the spring
in which uncleanness itself can be purified,
the spring of the house of David
which gushes up unflaggingly
to wash away sin
and the waste of the womb alike.[1]

And the mother of all purity
has seemed to be purified by the law
so as to show forth
at one and the same time
the strength of all-obedient humility
and the truth of the Gospel's purifying power.

Where is the human being
so stubbornly and mistakenly presumptuous of his
own holiness
as to refuse to undergo the cleansing action
of the remedy of penance?

Even if he really be holy
surely he cannot be as holy as she,
the most holy of all the holy,
Mary
who gave birth to the Holy of Holies.

Guerric of Igny[2]

[1] Zech 13:1

[2] First Sermon for the Feast of
the Purification, 1

For me this gathering is indeed
a matter for celebration
for me this procession is an occasion
for solemnity
and every kind of festal joy.

On the one hand
there come the Child and his mother
Jesus and Mary.

On the other hand,
coming to meet them
are the old man and the widow,
Simeon and Anna.

On the one hand
the Lord and the Lady.
On the other hand
the servant and the handmaid.

On the one hand
the Mediator and the mediatrix
the Son and the Mother.

On the other hand
such faithful and devout witnesses
and ministers to them.

In this gathering
—finally—
mercy and truth have met[1]
that is,
the merciful redemption of Jesus
and the truthful witness of the old man and woman.

In this meeting
justice and peace have kissed[2]
when the justice of the devout old man and woman
and the peace of him who reconciles the world
were united in the kiss of their affections and in
spiritual joy ✍

Nazareth rejoiced at the annunciation
Bethlehem at the nativity;
do you too rejoice, Jerusalem,
at the purification,
for he who was conceived at Nazareth
and born at Bethlehem
was welcomed and proclaimed at Jerusalem. ✍

Guerric of Igny [3]

[1] Ps 85:10
[2] Ibid.
[3] Sermon 16.6: Second Sermon for the Feast of the Purification,

Consider the four illustrious persons
in this procession:
those whose life not only lights up the churches
but also adorns the heavens.
I mean
Jesus and Mary
Simeon and Anna.

And to go from the lower to the higher:
in Anna
who served God by night and by day
in fasting and prayer[1]
fasting and prayer are recommended to us.

In Simeon
who embraced Jesus with such joy:
piety and devotion.

In Mary
who although she owed nothing to the Law as regards
purification
none the less fulfilled the Law:
humility and obedience.

In the Lord Jesus
who, born of a woman, was also born under the Law
in order to redeem those who were under the Law:[2]
charity and mercy ☙

Let us then pray to him
with the merits alike
of the Virgin Mary
and of Simeon and Anna
to intercede for us
that he may grant us
the virtue we lack
and watch over what he has granted,
so that through his watchful care
we may keep his deposit intact
and when we return it to him
may obtain the reward he gives.

Guerric of Igny[3]

[1] Lk 2:37
[2] Gal 4:4f
[3] Sermon 16.7: Second Sermon for the Feast of the Purification

Close to my heart shall he lodge
it is written.[1]

And even when I give him back
to his mother
he shall remain with me.

And when he is snuggled
close to his mother's heart
he shall still linger close to mine.

My heart, too, will be drunk
with the overflow of his loving-kindness,
though not so much as his mother's.

For she is the one-only Mother of Mercy All High
so that in a wonderful way
she is fruitful
with the fruitfulness of divine mercy.

O Full of Grace
you I congratulate and praise.

You gave birth
to the Loving-kindness I received.
You gave shape
to the candle I accepted.
You prepared the wax
for the touch of the light,
O Virgin,
Virgin of Virgins
when
as the unblemished mother
you clothed in unblemished flesh
the unblemishable Word.

Guerric of Igny [2]

[1] Sg 1:12
[2] Sermon 15.3: First Sermon for the Feast of the Purification

His Mother Pondered All These Things in Her Heart

Now his parents went to Jerusalem every year at the feast of the Passover. And when he was twelve years old, they went up according to custom; and when the feast was ended, as they were returning, the boy Jesus stayed behind in Jerusalem. His parents did not know it, but supposing him to be in the company they went a day's journey, and they sought him among their kinsfolk and acquaintances; and when they did not find him, they returned to Jerusalem, seeking him. After three days they found him in the temple, sitting among the teachers, listening to them and asking them questions; and all who heard him were amazed at his understanding and his answers. And when they saw him they were astonished; and his mother said to him, 'Son, why have you treated us so? Behold, your father and I have been looking for you anxiously.' And he said to them, 'How is it that you sought me? Did you not know that I must be in my Father's house?' And they did not understand the saying which he spoke to them. And he went down with them and came to Nazareth, and was obedient to them; and his mother pondered all these things in her heart. And Jesus increased in wisdom and in stature, and in favor with God and man.

Luke 2:40-52

Picture to yourself
what great sorrow
befell the Virgin
when she realized she had lost her Son,
what anguish
crushed those very bowels of mercy
when she did not see the Beloved of her womb.

Picture the great solicitude
with which she sought him
whom she loved above all else.[1]

And picture
how great
was the happiness
that overflooded her heart
when
—at the end of three days—
she saw him
whom she loved to the very depths of her soul
sitting in the midst of the learned
listening to them
and asking them questions. [2]

O blessed and most loving of virgins,
what must have been going through your soul
when you heard with your own ears
the young boy Jesus
expounding the law
to legal experts and men of learning,
discussing the non-observance of the Law
with great erudition,
and when you heard him disseminating
the salutary teachings of the New Law
and excelling in amazing debating skills.

What answer can be given to all this
beyond what is said in these words of the Gospel:
*Mary treasured all these things
and pondered on them in her heart.*[3]

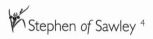
Stephen *of* Sawley [4]

[1] Sg 3:4
[2] Lk 2:46
[3] Lk 2:19
[4] Ninth Meditation on the Joys of the Virgin Mary

How is it,
my dear Lord,
that you did not have compassion
on your most holy Mother
as she looked for you,
grieved for you,
sighed for you?
For she and your father looked for you in sorrow.[1]

Why did you,
my dearest Lady,
look for the boy
who you well knew was God?

Were you afraid that he might be
tormented by hunger,
harassed by cold,
or suffer from wrong from a boy of his own age?

Is it not he who feeds and nourishes all things,
who clothes and adorns more gloriously than
Solomon
the grass of the field
which is there today and tomorrow
is cast into the fire? [2]

Indeed, my Lady
—if you will allow me to say so—
why did you lose your dearest Son so easily
why did you watch over him with such little care
why were you so late in noticing that he was missing?

Tell me,
my dearest Lady,
Mother of my Lord,
what were your feelings
your surprise
your joy
when you found your dearest son
the boy Jesus
not among boys but among teachers,
and beheld the gaze of all eyes bent on him,
everyone eagerly listening to him,
while the little and the great,
the learned and the ignorant
alike
told of his wisdom and of the answers he gave?

I found him, she says,
him whom my soul loves.
I held him fast
and would not let him go.[3]

Hold him fast,
dearest lady,
hold fast him whom you love,
cast yourself upon his neck,
embrace him,
kiss him,
and make up for his absence during three days
with increased delight.

Son,
why have you behaved so to us?
Behold, your father and I have been looking for you in sorrow.[4]

Again, I ask you,
my Lady,
why did you grieve?

It was, I think,
not of hunger or thirst or lack of food
that you were afraid for the boy
who you knew was God.

It was only that you could not bear to be deprived
even for a while
of the ineffable delights you found
in his presence.

For the Lord Jesus
is so dear to those who have some experience of him,
so beautiful to those who look upon him,
so sweet to those who embrace him,
that a short absence on his part
gives rise to the greatest pain.

How is it that you sought me?
he asked.
Did you not know
that I must be concerned with my Father's business?[5]

Here already
he begins to disclose
the secret of the heavenly mysteries
in which he had been occupied for the three days....

But what is the meaning of the Evangelist's statement:
they did not understand what he said to them?[6]
This does not, I think,
apply to Mary,
for from the moment
the Holy Spirit came upon her
and the power of the Most High overshadowed her[7]
she could not be ignorant
of any purpose of her Son.

While the rest did not understand what he had said,
Mary
knowing and understanding
kept all these things in her heart and pondered them.[8]

She kept them by the exercise of memory,
she pondered them in her meditation,
and she compared them
with the other things
which she had seen and heard of him.

So the most blessed Virgin
was even then making merciful provision for us,
in order that matters so sweet,
so wholesome,
so necessary,
might not through some neglect
be lost of memory
and therefore not written down or proclaimed,
with the result
that his followers would be deprived
of such delightful spiritual manna.

This most prudent virgin
therefore
faithfully preserved all these things,
modestly remained silent,
then
when the time came
told of them
and entrusted them to the holy apostles and disciples
to be preached.

Aelred *of* Rievaulx[9]

[1] Lk 2:48
[2] Mt 6:29f
[3] Song 3:4
[4] Lk 2:48
[5] Lk 2:49
[6] Lk 2:50
[7] Lk 1:35
[8] Lk 2:51
[9] On Jesus at the Age of Twelve, 1.2, 8-9

She sought her Son in Jerusalem.

He was twelve years old in his humanity;
according to his divinity
his years neither pass
nor pass away.[1]

In testimony to his real incarnation
she used appropriate maternal authority
saying
Child,
why have you treated us like this?
Behold, your father and I have been seeking you in sorrow.[2]

And although he spoke of a far different Father[3]
—for his is a two-fold nature—
he showed himself obedient:
the Lord
to his servants
the Creator
to his creatures.

Geoffrey *of* Auxerre [4]

[1] Ps 102:27
[2] Lk 2:48
[3] Lk 2:49
[4] Sermon 14 on the Apocalypse

Who else would dare
as Mary did,
to call 'son'
the Lord and God of angels
and to say,
son, why have you treated us so?[1]

Would any angel dare this?
They already consider it a great favor
to be called
and to be
angels,
when they are no more than spirits,
as David suggests when he says,
He makes the spirits his angels.[2]

Yet this was the same Majesty
whom they serve with awe and reverence [3]
that Mary,
—knowing herself the mother—
confidently called
her son.

Nor did God disdain
to be called
what he had deigned
to become.

As the Evangelist tells us a bit later:
he was obedient to them.[4]

Who?
God.

To whom?
To human beings.

God,
I repeat
to whom the angels are subject
whom the principalities and the powers obey,[5]
was obedient
to Mary.

And not only to Mary
but to Joseph, too,
for Mary's sake.
Marvel then
at these two things:
the gracious kindness of the Son
and the surpassing dignity of the mother.

Choose which you consider more wonderful.

Just imagine.
A double marvel.

God does what a woman says:
unheard of humility.

A woman outranks God:
unparalleled sublimity.

In praise of the virgins we sing:
they follow the Lamb wherever he goes.[6]

Of what praise then do you consider her worthy,
who preceded him?

Bernard *of* Clairvaux [7]

[1] Lk 2:48
[2] Ps 104:4
[3] Heb 12:28
[4] Lk 2:51
[5] Col 2:15
[6] Rev 14:4
[7] Homily One in Praise of the Blessed Virgin Mary, 6-7

The books
of the apostles and the orthodox fathers
are full of comparisons of figure and truth,
and they demonstrate
the harmony of the two testaments
so that the reason for faith
may more clearly
be revealed.

So whether we compare
words with words,
or words and works with works,
all is found to be in harmony
with what is written
in both testaments
of Christ.

And something that is seen to be corroborated
by such agreement in testimony
cannot be weakened
by any contradiction.

Zachariah speaks of the comparison of testimonies:
Blessed be the Lord God of Israel,
for he has visited his people
and brought about their redemption.
He has raised up a horn of salvation for us
in the house of his servant David,
as he spoke by the mouth of his holy prophets from of old.[1]

Of this comparison it is written:
Mary kept all these words, pondering them in her heart.[2]

What did she keep in her heart,
if not what she herself had seen and heard,
either from the things that had been foretold
by the prophets,
or from what had been announced to the shepherds
by the angels,
or from what the shepherds themselves
had reported to others?

Of this comparison
she herself says:
He has received his servant Israel,
being mindful of his mercy,
as he spoke to our fathers,
Abraham and his seed for ever.[3]

Baldwin *of* Forde [4]

[1] Lk 1:68-70
[2] Lk 2:19
[3] Lk 1:54-55
[4] The Commendation of Faith, 90.6-7

They Have No Wine

On the third day there was a marriage at Cana in Galilee, and the mother of Jesus was there; Jesus also was invited to the marriage, with his disciples. When the wine failed, the mother of Jesus said to him, 'They have no wine'. And Jesus said to her, 'Woman, what have you to do with me? My hour has not yet come'. His mother said to the servants, 'Do whatever he tells you'.

Now six stone jars were standing there, for the Jewish rites of purification, each holding twenty or thirty gallons. Jesus said to them, 'Fill the jars with water'. And they filled them up to the brim. He said to them, 'Now draw some out, and take it to the steward of the feast'. So they took it. When the steward of the feast tasted the water now become wine, and did not know where it came from (though the servants who had drawn the water knew), the steward of the feast called the bridegroom and said to him, 'Every man serves the good wine first; and when men have drunk freely, then the poor wine; but you have kept the good wine until now'.

John 2:1-10

When the wine failed at the marriage feast,
the mother of Jesus said briefly
to her Lord and Son
They have no wine.[1]

She obviously believed
that to have mentioned the matter
was all that was needed.

She spoke of the lack,
and meanwhile refrained from petition,
unless in fact the desire
of that heart,
so worthy of reverence,
sounded more loudly in his ears
than any petition.

All desire,
above all one so holy,
is very eloquent.

So the bride of the Word of God
believes that
when she is with her almighty spouse
she has no need at all
of busying herself
with the exigencies of petition.

She is in his possession,
and the most powerful reason for being cured
is that she is somebody
who languishes
for his love.

John of Ford [2]

[1] Jn 11:3
[2] Sermon One on the Song of Songs, 4

When the wine gave out,
the Mother of Jesus said to him,
'They have no wine.' [1]

Being merciful,
being kind through and through,
she felt compassion for their embarrassment.

What issues from the fountain of loving-kindness[2]
if not loving-kindness?

Is it any wonder then
if the bowels of loving-kindness
exhibit loving-kindness?

If someone's hand holds an apple for half a day,
does it not retain the scent of the apple
for the rest of the day?

How much then
did the power of loving-kindness
affect the womb in which it rested for nine months?

It filled her mind
before it filled her body,
and when it proceeded from her womb
it did not recede from her mind.

The Lord's reply
may seem somewhat harsh and severe,
but he knew to whom he was speaking
and she had no doubt
who was speaking to her.

That you may know how she received his answer
and how much she counted on her Son's goodness,
she told the servants,
Do whatever he tells you.[3]

Bernard *of* Clairvaux [4]

[1] Jn 2:3
[2] *Pietas*
[3] Jn 2:5
[4] First Sermon for the First Sunday after the Octave of Epiphany, 2

At a wedding in Galilee
she pitied the couple's embarrassment
and as the mother of mercy
simply suggested to her son:
They have no wine.[1]

She was content to mention
the need for kindness
to the One
who understands the needy and the poor.[2]

The last words of the Virgin in the Gospel
were addressed to the servants
at the wedding.

She advised them
to keep and to do
whatever the Lord might tell them, [3]
if he should say something.

'Excuse me'
[she said]
'from further explanation
because he of whom it was written
*The voice of the Lord is over the waters
the God of majesty thunders* [4]
meets every need.
Listen to him!'

That word
had its effect among the servants.

When they drew water
at the Saviour's command,
those who were complaining of the lack of wine
filled water jars in place of wine jars
preparing baths in place of drinks.

But they had not yet tested
the power of the One giving the command
for this was the first of his signs.[5]

 Geoffrey of Auxerre [6]

[1] Jn 2:3
[2] Cf Ps 41:1
[3] Jn 2:5

[4] Ps 29:3
[5] Jn 2:11
[6] Sermon 14 on the Apocalypse

How often, dear brothers,
after your tearful complaints
must I beseech the mother of Mercy
to point out to her gracious Son
that you have no wine?

And I assure you, beloved,
that if we lovingly urge it on her
she will not fail us in our need.

She is merciful
and the mother of mercy.

Now if she took pity
on the embarrassment of those who had invited her,
much more will she pity us
if we lovingly call on her.

Our wedding pleases her.
It concerns her far more than that other one,
since it was from her womb
—as from a wedding chamber—
that the heavenly bridegroom came forth. [1]

Yet who is not upset
that at that wedding
the Lord answered
his most gracious and holy mother
by saying,
Woman, what is that to me and to you?

And what is it
to you and to her,
Lord,
to a child and to his mother?

Why do you ask
what you have to do with her,
when you are the blessed fruit
of her immaculate womb?

Did she not conceive you
with her modesty intact,
and bear you
without harm [to her virginity]?

Did you not
spend nine months in her womb,
suck at her virginal breasts,
and at twelve years old
go down from Jerusalem with her,
and be subject to her?

Now, Lord,
why do you trouble her and say,
What is that to me and to you?

Much in every way.[2]

Now I see clearly
that you did not say,
What is that to me and to you
as if you were displeased,
or as wanting to disturb
your virgin mother's tender modesty.

No,
when the servants came to you
at your mother's bidding,
you did not put off doing
what she was prompting you to do.

Bernard *of* Clairvaux [3]

The fullness of grace
cannot consist in virginity alone
for not everyone can receive it with her.

Happy are they
who have not defiled their garments[1]
and
with our queen
glory in the privilege of virginity.

But have you only one blessing,[2]
O Lady?

Then
I implore
that you bless me!

Virtue has gone from me
I cannot even aspire to it.

I am rotting in my own filth
and have become like a beast;[3]
shall I then have no part with you?
Is there nowhere that I may be with you
because I lack the strength to follow you
wherever you go? [4]

The angel sought out the girl
whom the Lord prepared
for her Lord's son. [5]

He drank from your water pot
delighted at the virtue he recognized,
will you not give a drink as well to the beasts?

The angel drank
because you had not known a man; [6]
let the beasts drink as well
because you take delight uniquely
in your humility.

The Lord
—she says—
has regarded the lowliness
of his handmaiden.

Now virginity without humility
may always have glory,
but not with God. [7]
The Most High
always regards humility.
To the humble he gives grace,
the proud he resists. [8]

Yet perhaps
even with these two measures
your water pot is not yet full.[9]

Of yet a third is it capable,
so that not only the angel and the beasts may drink
but also the master of the feast. [10]

For this good wine
—which we have kept until now—
the ministering angel draws
to take to the master of the feast.

The Father,
I mean,
the First Person of the Trinity
who is rightly called the master of the feast.

Surely
in commending the fruitfulness of Mary
—which is that third measure—
the angel says:
The Holy One who will be born from you
will be called the Son of God.[11]
as if he were saying:
With him alone
have you this birth in common.

Bernard *of* Clairvaux [12]

[1] Rev 3:4
[2] Gen 27:38
[3] Ps 72:23
[4] Rev 14:4
[5] Gen 24:14
[6] Lk 1:34
[7] Rom 4:2
[8] Prv 3:34 LXX, Jm 4:6, 1 P 5:5
[9] Jn 2:6
[10] Jn 2:6-10
[11] Lk 1:35
[12] Sixth Sermon for the Assumption and Occasional Sermon 46

Blessed are They
Who Hear the Word of God
and Keep It

As Jesus was speaking, a woman in the crowd raised her voice and said to him, 'Blessed is the womb that bore you, and the breasts that you sucked!' But he said, 'Blessed rather are those who hear the word of God and keep it!'

Luke 11:27-28

Now as they went on their way, Jesus entered a village; and a woman named Martha received him into her house. And she had a sister called Mary, who sat at the Lord's feet and listened to his teaching. But Martha was distracted with much serving; and she went to him and said, 'Lord, do you not care that my sister has left me to serve alone? Tell her then to help me.' But the Lord answered her, 'Martha, Martha, you are anxious and troubled about many things; one thing is needful. Mary has chosen the good portion, which shall not be taken away from her.'

Luke 10:38-42

Yesterday[1]
it was read out
how *a certain woman* said to our Lord:
Blessed
is the womb that bore you and the breasts you suckled.

And the Lord said to her:
Rather blessed are those
who hear the word of God
and keep it.[2]

Let us therefore make ready a spiritual castle[3]
that our Lord may come to us.

If the Blessed Mary
had not prepared this castle within herself
–I dare say–
the Lord Jesus would not have entered her womb
or her spirit
nor would this Gospel be read on her feast today.. .

Three things make a castle strong:
a moat,
a wall
and a tower.

What is a moat
but deep ground?

Therefore
let us hollow out our heart
that it may be very low ground.

The earth
that we should take
and mound up
is our earthly fragility.

Let this not lie hidden within
but let it always be before our eyes
so that in our hearts
there may be a moat
—that is, low-lying and deep ground.

This moat, brothers,
is humility.

And unless this moat
—that is, true humility—
is first established in our heart,
we shall only be able to build something
that will fall in ruins about our head.

How well
the blessed Mary
had made this moat for herself!

Truly she was mindful
more of her own fragility
than of all her dignity and holiness.

She knew full well
that her fragility came from herself,
that her holiness,
that her being the Mother of God,
that her being the lady of the angels
and the temple of the Holy Spirit,
came only by God's grace.

Therefore, what she was of herself
she humbly confessed,
saying:
Behold the handmaid of the Lord.
Be it done unto me according to your word.[4]

And again:
He has looked upon the humility of his maidservant.[5]

Aelred *of* Rievaulx [6]

[1] In the Gospel of the vigil Mass.
[2] Lk 11:27-28
[3] *castellum*. The latin word can mean both village and castle. The Gospel of the day uses it in the former sense, but here Bernard uses it in the latter sense to develop his spiritual teaching. The analogy was widely used by later writers, the best known of whom is Teresa of Avila.
[4] Lk 1:38
[5] Lk 1:48.
[6] Sermon 19.5-6, 9: On the Feast of the Assumption.

After the moat
we must make the wall.
This spiritual wall is chastity ✍

Holy Mary
had this wall within herself
more perfectly than anyone else.
For she is the holy and untouched virgin.

Her virginity
—like the stoutest of walls—
could never be penetrated
by any projectile
or by any other instrument
—that is, by any temptation of the devil.

She was a virgin before giving birth,
a virgin in giving birth,
and a virgin after giving birth.

Yet, even if you are already imitating
the most blessed Mary
and have this moat of humility
and the wall of chastity,
it is essential
that you build the tower of charity ✍

Who can say how perfectly
the most blessed Mary had this tower?

If Peter loved
his Lord,
how much did the Blessed Mary love
her Lord and her Son!

How much she loves her neighbors
—that is, [all] men and women—
is demonstrated
by the many miracles
and the many visions
by which the Lord has deigned to show
that she prays for the whole human race
in a special way to her Son.

It would be superfluous
for me to try to show
even the beginnings of her charity. ♫

This is without a doubt the castle
which Jesus deigns to enter. ♫
This is the castle
which Jesus did enter.

He entered
with the gate shut
and with the gate shut
he exited
—as the holy Ezekiel had foretold:
*He brought me round to the gate that faced eastward
and it was shut.*[1]

The east gate
is Mary most holy.

For the gate which faces east
generally receives the brightness of the sun first.

So Mary most blessed
—who always looked to the east,
to the brightness of God—
first received within herself
the ray,
indeed the whole fullness of the brightness
of the true sun
—the Son of God,
of whom Zachary said:
The Rising Sun visited us from on high.[2]

The gate was closed and well secured.[3]

The enemy could find no entrance,
absolutely no opening.

It was closed
and sealed with the seal of chastity
which was not broken
but rather made more solid and firmer
by the entrance of the Lord.

For the One who gives the gift of virginity
did not by his presence
take virginity away
but rather confirmed it.

Therefore, *into* this *castle Jesus entered.*[4]

And we,
if we have within us this spiritual castle
of which we speak,
without a doubt Jesus will spiritually enter into us.

But he entered into the Blessed Mary
not only spiritually
but also physically
because
in her
and from her
he took a physical body.

Aelred *of* Rievaulx [5]

[1] Ezk 44:1; cfr. 47:2
[2] Lk 1:78
[3] Ez 44:1-2; Jos 6:1
[4] Lk 10:38
[5] Sermon 19:10-17: On the Feast of the Assumption

Saint Benedict
 or rather the Holy Spirit in Saint Benedict
did not say and decree that we
like Mary,
be intent only on *lectio*,[1]
and lay aside work,
like Martha,
but he commended both to us,
allotting certain times to Martha's work
and certain times to Mary's work.

In the Blessed Mary,
our Lady,
these two activities were perfectly present.

The fact that she clothed our Lord,
that she fed him,
that she carried him
and fled with him into Egypt
—all this pertains to physical activity.

But that *she treasured all these words,*
pondering them in her heart,[2]
that she meditated on his divinity,
contemplated his power,
and savored his sweetness—
all this pertains to Mary.

Accordingly, the Evangelist beautifully says:
Mary,
sitting at the feet of Jesus,
listened to his word.[3]

In the role of Martha,
Blessed Mary did not sit *at Jesus' feet.*
Instead, I should think,
the Lord Jesus himself sat at the feet of his dearest
mother.
For, as the Evangelist says: *He was subject to them,*[4]
that is, to Mary and Joseph.

But in that she saw and recognized his divinity,
beyond doubt she sat at his feet,
for she humbled herself before him
and reckoned herself as his handmaid.

In the role of Martha,
she tended him
as someone weak and small,
hungry and thirsty;
she grieved at his sufferings
and at the outrages which the Jews heaped on him.

This is why she is told:
Martha, Martha,
you are troubled and anxious about many things.[5]

In the role of Mary,
she entreated him as Lord,
worshiped him as Lord,
and yearned with all her might
for his spiritual sweetness.

Aelred *of* Rievaulx [6]

[1] meditative, prayerful reading
[2] Lk 2:19
[3] Lk 10:39
[4] Lk 2:51
[5] Lk 10:41
[6] Sermon 19.22-24: On the Feast of the Assumption

After her Son ascended
to where he was before[1]
the mother
—released from all temporal anxiety
and more fully enlightened by the Holy Spirit—
–for besides the special first grace
which she received at the incarnation,
she received him in common with the apostles—
rejoiced
to be still
and to see[2]
that Jesus is God.

A vision of wholly ineffable joy and supreme delight
for all who love Jesus[3]
but above all others
for her
who gave birth to Jesus
–for as the grace of giving birth to God
was conferred on her apart from all others
so was the privilege of glorying in him
to whom she gave birth.

Altogether her own
and without comparison
was the glory of the Virgin Mother,
to see God the King of all
in the diadem of the flesh
with which she crowned him,[4]
to recognize God
and to adore him
in her own body
and see her own body
glorified in God.

These are the truths which here below
Mary rejoiced to contemplate.
This is the best part,
which she had chosen,
which today has not been taken away from her
but has been brought to perfection in her.[5]

Guerric of Igny [6]

[1] Jn 6:63
[2] Cf. Ps 45:11
[3] 1 Cor 2:9
[4] Cf Sg 3:11
[5] Lk 10:42
[6] Sermon 50.3: Fourth Sermon for the Feast of the Assumption

The praise of true beauty
belongs to the mind rather than the body. ⚘

This interior beauty loves regularity and balance.
For where there is no cause for irregularity,
irregularity is always unseemly...

In the case of the Virgin,
we are looking for the precise way
in which the features of her face are proportioned,
for [her face] is so attractive and so praiseworthy
that a more attractive or more praiseworthy
cannot be found among all the daughters of Sion.[1]

And in what better way
can we speak of the regularity of her features
than in the balance of humility and honor,
of condescension and dignity?

It is written:
The greater you are,
the more you should humble yourself in all things. [2]
If you stand out from the crowd,
become one of the crowd,
if you are always in command,
do not think it beneath you to be subservient.

Baldwin *of* Forde [3]

[1] Sg 3:11
[2] Si 3:20
[3] Tractate 7

Mary has chosen the best part. [1]

The best, surely,
for the fruitfulness of marriage is good
but the chastity of a virgin is better.
And it follows that the best of all
is virginal fruitfulness
or fruitful virginity.

This is the privilege of Mary. [2]
It is given to no other,
for *it shall not be taken away from her.* [3]

It is unique
yet it is inexpressible
so no one can achieve it
nor can anyone describe it.

What if you go on to ask:
Whose mother?

What tongue
even that of an angel,
can worthily extol the praises of the Virgin Mother,
the mother of not just anyone
but of God?

Twofold is the newness
twofold the prerogative
twofold the miracle
yet fittingly and worthily applied to her.

No other son adorned the virgin
nor any other birth adorn God.

Bernard *of* Clairvaux [4]

[1] Lk 10:42
[2] Is 42:8
[3] Lk 10:42
[4] Sermon Four for the Feast of the Assumption, 5

Who is this
who makes her way up
from the desert
brimming with delights ?[1]

These delights
are the fruit of virtue
and while they sprout or flower
or are merely immature
they are mixed
with a certain bitterness
with difficulty and distress;
but through these things
at the last
they yield the sweetest and most tranquil
fruit of justice

Just as when a thing has ripened
and the husk or shell has been discarded
and one gets to the sweetness and delights of the
kernel
and something that has long been in preparation
is finally plucked
with contentment and gladness:

similarly
once this life is over
and all our hard work at the virtues has been set aside
we shall delight in the virtues themselves
pure and simple.

It was in virtue
that the blessed Virgin Mary excelled
above all others
during her earthly life
—and so it was that
she conceived directly by the Holy Spirit
at Nazareth.

Now
in the heavenly realm
—in the true House of Bread[2]—
she brims over with absolute delight
far more abundantly than all others
as she forever leans
on her Beloved [3]
on him
whom she bore more
with faith and love
in her heart
than in her flesh
as is clear from these words:
Blessed are those who hear the word of God and keep it.

 Isaac of Stella [4]

[1] Sg 8:5
[2] Bethlehem, see Jerome, Letter 108.10
[3] Sg 8:5
[4] Sermon 52.6: Second Sermon for the Feast of the Assumption

Standing by the Cross

S tanding by the cross of Jesus were his mother, and his mother's sister, Mary the wife of Clopas, and Mary Magdalene. When Jesus saw his mother, and the disciple whom he loved standing near, he said to his mother, 'Woman, behold, your son!' Then he said to the disciple, 'Behold, your mother!' And from that hour the disciple took her to his own home.

John 19:25-27

There stood by the cross of Jesus
his mother, Mary
and his mother's sister,
Mary Cleophas,
and Mary Magdalen.

The disciple whom Jesus loved
stood there also
close beside the Lord's mother.

To *stand by the cross* of Jesus
seems to me an act of the very highest worth.

To *stand by the cross of Jesus*
means to be
with the blessed mother of Jesus
and the bride of the Word
and with the companions of his bride
and to lift one's eyes to the crucified
fixing them there
pondering
on these treasures of immense love
with a very deep sense of devotion.

If only
there were some way
by which we too
could become worthy
of being counted among this company,
of being sharers in their blessedness.

Yet the name 'mother' or 'bride'
may be applied quite justly
to anyone
who is moved by motherly affection
to bring forth
and to train sons for God,
to anyone
who has entered completely
into the pure love of the Word,
and so cried to the Father
with ceaseless longing:
Let him kiss me with the kiss of his mouth. [1]

If anyone is blessed
with both these gifts,
so that
zeal for his brothers' salvation
is no hindrance at all
to the exercise of divine love;
and love for God
is no obstacle
to the duty of saving others,
then that person
is not simply blessed
but manifestly very specially and greatly blessed.

A person like this
has won a place
next to the cross of Jesus,
a very close place,
one next to the Lord's mother,
who was both mother and bride
to the only Son of God.

John of Ford [2]

[1] Sg 1:1
[2] Sermon 26 on the Song of Songs, 4-5

Who can rightly fathom
the Mother's sorrow
when she saw the precious body
of her Son
which she knew was
utterly holy and free of all blemish
stretched out on the wood of a cross
and the head of Jesus
in whose presence the angels trembled
crowned with thorns
or when she saw his hands and feet
pierced with nails
his side
split wide open by a soldier's lance
and a flow of blood running down
on every part of his body?

Truly
mother most loving,
the word of his suffering pierced through your soul.[1]
yet despite being wounded
to the very depth of your being
by a sorrow
without comparison and beyond description
you stood there
as he hung from the cross
and witnessed how so powerful, innocent, good and
loving a Son
was put to so horrible a death.

You saw him
lashed savagely by torturers.
You saw
how irreverently
he was reckoned among thieves.[2]

And yet
despite your great anguish and sorrow
did you not think of mercy
–his mercy–
as he redeemed you and the whole world?

Did you not rejoice
with unbounded happiness
knowing with a faith that was certain and
unshakeable
that your Son's precious blood
had redeemed the whole world;
that hell had been despoiled;
that the devil
—though strong—
had been chained;
and that the door to the kingdom of heaven
had been thrown wide open?

Did you not rejoice
when you heard his tender voice
entrusting you to John
–his beloved disciple–
so that a girgin would care
for his virgin mother?

For whom did he value more
among those he left behind in his world
than John
to whose love he could entrust
so priceless a treasure
of our hope and salvation?

Stephen *of* Sawley [3]

[1] Lk 2:35
[2] Lk 22:37
[3] Meditation Eleven on the Sorrows of the Virgin Mary

She stood by Jesus' cross
as the pain of the cross
crucified her mind
and a sword pieced her own soul[1]
as she beheld
the body of her Son
pierced with wounds.

Rightly therefore
was she recognized there
as his Mother
and by his care
entrusted to a suitable protector.

In this
both the mother's unalloyed love for her Son
and the Son's kindness toward his Mother
were proven to the utmost.

On other occasions
he seemed almost to ignore his Mother:
whether
at the wedding feast
when she asked for a miracle
and he answered:
'No, woman.
Why do you trouble me with that?'[2]

And again:
in the midst of his preaching the Gospel
when someone told him:
'Behold, your mother and your brothers
are standing outside,
asking for you.'

And he answered,
'Who is my mother?'[3]

Yet he had to give such an answer:

to his mother
when she asked for a miracle
in order to show that miracles came to him
not from his mother
but from another source;

and to the man
who interrupted the words of the Gospel
by announcing his relatives
in order to demonstrate that spiritual things
must come before those of the flesh.

It was as if
—as in the same way as earlier—
he were saying
to his relative seeking him
while he was busy with the work of the Gospel:
'Why do you seek me?
Do you not know
that I must be about my Father's business?'[4]

That he spurned his Mother
—he who so carefully laid down the law
that parents should be honored[5] —
could not be.

That on earth
he showed disgust for his mother
when from heaven
he had desired her beauty
could not be.

But instead,
both by his words
and by his example
he was setting charity in order in us[6]
teaching us
to put before our affection for physical attachments
not only the love of God
but also the love of those who do God's will.

For the affection
which is demanded from the hearts
of all of us
whom the supreme Father has deigned to adopt[7]
is one which will cause us to say
in faith
together with his Only-begotten:
'Whoever
does the will of my Father who is in heaven
is my brother
and my sister
and my mother.'[8]

These words apply indeed
to God's children.

Nor does the Spirit himself
bear any more faithful witness to our spirit
that we are God's children
than that this utterance of God's Only-begotten
should sound from our hearts.

Jesus demonstrates that Mary
who was his mother according to the flesh
is his mother in another way as well,
because she too so valued the Father's will
that the Father could foretell to her:
'You shall be called "My Will is in Her" ' .[9]

Therefore:
when the Son seemed to ignore her
then he is found to have honored her yet more,
for the honor of the name of mother
is doubled for her.

Now she bears in spirit
through inspiration
the same Son
whom she bore in her womb
through incarnation.

Guerric of Igny [10]

[1] Cf Lk 2:49
[2] Jn 2:4
[3] Mt 12:47f
[4] Lk 2:49.
[5] Ex 20:12; Mt 15:4
[6] Sg 2:4
[7] Rom 8:15
[8] Mt 12:50
[9] Is 62:4
[10] Sermon 50.1-2: Fourth Sermon on the Feast of the Assumption

Loving her as he did

Jesus loved her to the end[1]
not only bringing his life to an end for her
but also speaking almost his last words
for her benefit.

As his last will and testament
he committed to his beloved heir
the care of his mother
in whose debt he knew himself to be.

So Christ divided his inheritance
between Peter who loved the most
and John who was loved the most.

To Peter fell the Church
to John, Mary.[2]

This bequest belonged to John
not only by right of kinship
but also because of the privilege
love had bestowed
and the witness his chastity bore.

For it was appropriate
that only a virgin
should minister to the Virgin
so that
the blessed Virgin
languishing for love of God
should be stayed up with the flowers of chastity[3]
and the young man's virginity
should in the meantime
receive that much recompense

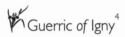Guerric of Igny[4]

[1] Jn 13:1
[2] Cf Jn 21:15, 19:26
[3] Sg 2:5

[4] Sermon 50.3: Fourth Sermon
for the Feast of the Assumption

Will your eyes be dry
as you see your most loving Lady
in tears?

Will you not weep
as her soul is pierced
by the sword of sorrow?[1]

Will there be no sob from you
as you hear Jesus say to his mother:
Woman, behold your son,
and to John
behold your mother? [2]

He entrusts his Mother to the disciple
and he promises the thief paradise.

Aelred *of* Rievaulx [3]

[1] Cf Lk 2:35
[2] Jn 19:26
[3] Rule of Life for a Recluse, 31

The martyrdom of the Virgin
—which, you may remember, we named
as the twelfth star in your crown—
is mentioned in the prophecy of Simeon
as well as in the account of the Lord's passion.

Behold, this child is set for a sign
which shall be spoken against[1]
says the holy old man
of the infant Jesus.

And to Mary he said:
And a sword shall pierce through your own soul too.[2]

Truly, blessed Mother,
a sword has pierced your soul.

Unless it pierced your soul
it would not penetrate the flesh of your Son.

And after your Jesus
—he belongs to all, but especially to you—
gave up his spirit
the cruel lance did not touch his soul.

It opened his side
—not sparing him even after death
although it could harm him no more—
but it pierced your soul.

His soul was not there;
but yours could not avoid it.

An agony of grief
therefore pierced your soul
and we may
—not without reason—
call you more than a martyr
in that the bond of your compassion
far exceeded physical suffering.[3]

Bernard *of* Clairvaux[4]

[1] Lk 2:34
[2] Lk 2:35
[3] In Latin: *passio* (suffering) and *compassio* (suffering with).
[4] Sermon for the Octave of the Feast of the Assumption, 14

Did Mary not know in advance
that Jesus would die?

Surely she did.

Did she not hope
that He would straightway rise again?

Assuredly she did.

Yet did she grieve
as he was crucified?

Bitterly she did.

Could he die
in the body
and she not die with him
in her heart?

A love[1]
greater than anyone possesses
brought this about.

A love
the like of which has not since been seen
after her.

Bernard of Clairvaux[2]

[1] Charitas
[2] Sermon for the Octave of the Assumption, 15

He has Exalted the Humble

And Mary said, 'My soul magnifies the Lord, and my spirit rejoices in God my Saviour, for he has regarded the low estate of his handmaiden. For behold, henceforth all generations will call me blessed; for he who is mighty has done great things for me, and holy is his name. . .he has put down the mighty from their thrones, and has exalted the humble and meek.'

Luke 1:46-49, 52

When Mary was about to depart
from the body
she took to her bed
as is the way with human weakness.

The daughters of the Jerusalem which is above[1]
—that is, the angelic powers—
well aware that the Son's favor is to be won
by attention shown to the Mother,
were then,
with dutifulness and devotion,
visiting their Lady,
the mother of their Lord.[2]

And perhaps,
after duly greeting her,
the angels
—adapting their language to human affections
as they adapted their appearance to a human form—
first spoke to her in some way such as this:

'Lady,
why is it, I beg,
that you seem so ill and faint?

'Why is it
that, unlike your wont,
you are sad and inactive,
that for some time now
you do not revisit the holy places
as you were accustomed to do,
feeding your love by contemplating them?

'For some days now
we have not seen you climbing the rock of Calvary
to flood the place of the cross with tears;
or at the tomb of your Son
worshipping the glory of his resurrection;
or on Mount Olivet
kissing the last traces he left as he ascended.'

For she is believed to have dwelt in the valley of
Josaphat
where her tomb is pointed out
—as Saint Jerome says—
in a church built with an extraordinary stone floor,
for this reason:
that she need not go far from the holy places
but may visit them often.

She kept everything in her memory
yet in this way
she tenderly embraced those events,
as it were, bodily portrayed
in the very places in which they had occurred,
and by this means at least to some extent
she consoled her love.

When therefore the angels inquire the reason
why she no longer does this
and has taken to her bed,
she says:
I languish.

'Why do you languish?
What place can languor claim in your body
in which the Health of the world for so long dwelt?
From the body of that Son of yours
went forth power
which healed everyone.[3]

'Even touching the hem of his garment
healed the woman with the issue of blood.[4]

'And you held him for such a long time
in your womb
in your bosom
on your lap.

'How, after that,
could you be liable
to any weakness or languor?'

'There is no reason why you should be surprised at
this,'
she says,
'If you remember how it once was with the body of
my Son.
I know how weak it was
and subject to how many needs,
although of his own free will.

'I know.
I who fed him in the womb
suckled him at my breasts
cherished him in my bosom
and saw the needs not only of his infancy
but also of subsequent periods in his life,
tending them as far as I could.

'At the end
it was not without suffering
that I beheld
the mockery and the torments
of his passion and cross,[5]
learning through them
one by one
how truly Isaiah spoke of him
when he said:
*Indeed he bore our ills
and himself carried our pains.*[6]

'Why should I grieve
that he has not given to my body
what he did not give to his own?

'I am not so softly nurtured
or so proud
that I cannot
or will not
suffer to some slight extent
what he saw fit to suffer.

'For him
it was a matter
of free will and compassion.
For me
of nature and necessity.

'Health is one thing,
holiness surely another.

'Holiness
he gave to my body
by the mystery of his body in its conception.

'Health
he promised to give after the pattern of his risen
body.

'In short,
that you may wonder less at my languor,
I languish with love.

'I languish
more from the impatience of love
than from suffering pain.

'I am more wounded
with charity
than weighed down by infirmity.'

'Alas,' they say,
'how frequent, indeed continual,
are the causes of your languor.'

'Good Jesus,
how this mother of yours languished
almost continually after giving birth to you.

'At first
she languished with fear,
afterwards with sorrow,
now with love.

'With fear
from your birth until your passion,
for she saw that the life of her Son
was always the object of scheming
and attempts at murder.

'With sorrow
throughout the time of the passion
until she recovered you
restored to life.

'Now she is tormented
more happily
but more pitifully
with love and desire
because she does not possess you as you sit in heaven.

'Good Jesus,
how have you,
who are the fruit of supreme joy,
become for her the cause
of so long a martyrdom;
that so many
and such sharp swords
pierce unceasingly
the soul dearest of all to you?[7]

'Lady,
we beg of you
what would you have us do for you?

'Do you wish at least that
Gabriel
—that companion in your initiation into the mystery
who from the beginning was aware of your secret
and ministered to it,
deserving also to be appointed guardian
of your chamber—
should stay here,
sit by you,
and wait on you?'

"There is no need for that'
she says.

'My virgin suffices for me,
the new angel in the flesh,
the disciple whom Jesus loved.[8]

'Of that love
He left me the heir
when on the cross he commended the disciple to me
and me to the disciple.[9]

'And nothing pleases me better
than his attentions,
since nothing could be more chaste
than his way of life and his affections,
nothing more delightful
than his behavior,
nothing more pure
than his faith,
nothing more holy
than his speech. '

When they went back
and told their Lord these things,
what shall we imagine Jesus said
if not something like this:

'It is I
who bade sons honor father and mother.[10]

'I who
in order to do what I taught
and to be an example to others,
went down to earth to honor my Father.

'Yet to honor my Mother,
I came back to heaven.
I came and prepared a placed for her,
a throne of glory,
where the queen might sit with the King
at his right hand
crowned and decked with golden-woven robes
of many colors.[11]

'And I say this
not in order that a throne be placed for her apart.
Rather she will be my throne.

'Come then,
my Chosen One,
and I will place my throne in you.

'In you
will I set up for myself a seat over my kingdom,
from you I will make judgements,
through you I will listen to prayers.

'No one ministered to me more
in my lowliness:
there is no one I want to minister to more plentifully
in my glory.

'To me
you imparted,
besides other things,
what makes me human.

'To you
I will impart
what makes me God.

'You implored the kiss of my mouth.
The whole of you will be kissed
by the whole of me.

'In an everlasting and indissoluble kiss
I will press
not my lips to your lips
but my spirit to your spirit.

'Because I have desired your beauty [12]
with greater longing even than you have desired
mine,
I shall not regard myself as sufficiently glorified
until you are glorified with me.'

'Glory to you,
Lord Jesus'
the choir of angels sang.

Glory to you,
Lord Jesus,
let the company of the faithful echo.

May the glorification of your mother
make for your glory,
and for our pardon.

May you grant this,
we pray,
You
to whom honor and glory belong
for ever and ever.
Amen.

Guerric *of* Igny [13]

[1] Gal 4:26
[2] Lk 1:43
[3] Cf Lk 6:19
[4] Mt 9:22ff.
[5] Jn 19:25
[6] Is 53:4
[7] Cf Lk 2:35

[8] Jn 21:20
[9] Jn 19:26f
[10] Mt 19:19; Ex 20:12
[11] Ps 44:10
[12] Ps 44:12
[13] Sermon 48: Second Sermon for the Feast of the Assumption

Our earth has today sent heaven
a precious gift,
that by giving and receiving
a happy compact of friendship
human affairs should be joined to divine
earthly with heavenly
and the lowest with the highest.

For the exalted fruit of the earth
has gone up
to the place[1]
whence all good and perfect gifts [2]
come down.

The Blessed Virgin
as she goes up on high therefore
will give these gifts to humankind.[3]

Why should she not?
She will lack neither the capacity
nor the will.

She is the queen of heaven
she is merciful.
And she is the mother of the Only-begotten Son of
God.

Nothing can so commend the greatness
of her power and loving-kindness.
And unless you somehow think
that the Son of God does not honor his mother
who can doubt
that the physical body of Mary
in which the Love of God lay bodily at rest
for nine months
has passed over into the bond of his love?

Bernard *of* Clairvaux [4]

[1] Is 4:2
[2] Jm 1:17
[3] Eph 4:8
[4] First Sermon for the Feast of the Assumption, 2

The ever blessed Mary
listened to this invitation
*Cross over to me
all you who crave me.*[1]

She listened to it
and she followed.

She crossed perfectly
over this sea of which we speak
and over the wall
and through the cloud.

Therefore she arrived perfectly
at that Wisdom
which cries out and says:
*Cross over to me
all you who crave me.*

This is why these words are read especially
on her solemnity.

She craved Christ;
therefore she passed over to Christ.

13

No one so perfectly
crossed over this sea
of which we have been speaking
as did blessed Mary.

She so perfectly crossed over
to Christ
in her heart
that Christ
crossed over to her
and remained with her
even in her body.

This is what Scripture means
that Aaron's sister
–who is named Mary–
led the sons of Israel
when they crossed over the Red Sea
and led them with a tambourine.[2]

Without doubt
the ever blessed Mary
–the true Mary,
whom the other Mary foreshadowed–
leads all who have crossed over this sea
–that is, the present world.

She leads the way in dignity
she leads in holiness
she leads in purity
and she also leads
in mortification of the flesh
–that is, with a tambourine.

She led in this as well:
she was the first of all of us
to cross over.

Aelred *of* Rievaulx [3]

[1] Si 24:26
[2] Ex 15:20
[3] Sermon 22.10, 14: On the Feast of the Nativity of Mary

You have welcomed me to glory. [1]

Today the Lord in heaven
welcomes the Mother
who welcomed him on earth
and she who welcomed him
to her womb
is welcomed by him
to his home.

No need to labor the point, is there?
In every case
welcome given
corresponds to
welcome gained;
just as rejection
corresponds to
rejection.

Mary's unique welcome
prepared her
for another unique welcome.

Martha had welcomed Christ to her home
Mary welcomed him to her womb.

Martha served him food of some kind or other
from somewhere[2]
Mary nursed her own Child
with her own milk.

Some women may have clothed him
with body-wear
Mary clothed him
with the body she bore.

Great sins were forgiven Mary of Magdala
because *she greatly loved,*
and *she greatly loved* [3]
because much had been forgiven her.

Mary was given
the very greatest gifts
because her love
was of the very greatest,
and she loves so exceedingly
because she has received so exceedingly.

Isaac *of* Stella [4]

[1] Ps 73:24
[2] Cf Lk 10:38ff
[3] Lk 7:47
[4] Sermon 53.10-11: Third Sermon for the Feast of the Assumption

Our queen has gone on before us
she has gone on before
and has been caught up so gloriously
that her servants may confidently follow their
mistress
crying:
Draw us after you.
We shall run in the odor of your ointments.[1]

An advocate
has been sent before us in our journey
and she who is the mother of the Jew
and the mother of pity
will transact the business of our salvation
effectively
and
with prayer.

Bernard *of* Clairvaux [2]

[1] Sg 1:3
[2] First Sermon for the Feast of the Assumption, 1

In all I sought rest.
Surely this is the voice of Wisdom.
It is the Church's voice.
It is Mary's voice.
It is the voice of any wise soul.

Wisdom
sought rest in all
but found it in the humble alone.

The Church
sought rest among all the nations of the world
but found it in believers alone.

Mary
like any faithful soul
sought rest in all her actions.

Today at last
she has found it
when
—after Herod's persecution and the flight into Egypt
after so many plots and outrages
on the part of the impious
after so much suffering
in her Son's passion and death
after so many and such sharp swords
piercing her soul—
at length today
she can say:
Return, my soul, to your rest
for the Lord has dealt generously with you. [1]

'He who created me
was created from me
and found rest in the tent of my body.[2]
He will not be able to refuse me
the rest of his heaven.
He heaps up grace for others.'

Continue, Mary, continue
free from anxiety
in the good things of your Son.
Act with full confidence
as queen,
the King's mother and bride.

You sought rest
but what is due to you
is of greater glory:
queenship and power.

He who shared with you
in one flesh and one spirit
the mystery of love and unity
–that is, when with due honor shown to nature
and through a twofold gift of grace
his Mother was united with him in matrimony–
wishes to share with you his realm.

Rest then,
happy
in the arms of the Bridegroom.

Guerric of Igny [3]

[1] Ps 116:7
[2] Cf. Sir 24:12
[3] Sermon 49.3: Third Sermon for the Assumption, 3

Today

as Mary enters the holy city[1]
she is carried by him
whom she had earlier carried
to a village of this world. [2]
But with what honor,
do you imagine:
what exultation
what glory?

In the world
there is no place more worthy
than the temple of the virgin womb
in which Mary carried the Son of God.

Nor in the heavens
than the royal throne
to which Mary's Son today
raises Mary.

Bernard *of* Clairvaux [3]

[1] Mt 27:53
[2] Lk 10:38
[3] First Sermon for the Feast of the Assumption, 3

Why is the Gospel reading in church today
about the woman
—blessed among all women[1] —
who carried the Saviour?

I believe that what we are celebrating
takes its value to some extent from that carrying,
so that alongside his inestimable glory
she too should be recognized as being inestimable.

For who
—even if he speaks with the
tongues of men and of angels[2] —
can explain how
by the operation of the Holy Spirit
by the overshadowing of the power of the Most High
the Word of God
—by whom all things were made[3] —
was made flesh; [4]
and the Lord of Majesty
—whom the created world cannot contain—[5]
enclosed himself within the virgin body
and was made man
and was enclosed within a virgin's womb?

Bernard *of* Clairvaux [6]

[1] Lk 10:38-42
[2] I Cor 13:1
[3] Jn 1:3
[4] Lk 1:35
[5] 3 Kgs [1 Kgs, Hebr.] 8:27
[6] First Sermon for the Feast of the Assumption, 3

When the mother of the incarnate Word
is taken up into heaven
it is a time for all flesh and blood to sing out loud,
and all humanity to utter praise without ceasing,
for in the Virgin
human nature is exalted above every immortal spirit.

But devotion does not permit us to be silent
about her glory
nor does mere thought conceive anything worthy,
nor can untaught speech give birth to it.

So it is that the celestial powers
when they see so rare a thing
cry out in admiration:
Who is she
who comes up from the wilderness
abounding in delights. [1]

As if they were to say more clearly:
'How great she is!
Whence abounds such richness of delights
on someone coming from the desert?
For such delights are not found among us
though we are made glad in the city of God
by flowing waters [2]
and though we drink in with glory
from the countenance of glory.

Who is she,
who rises from beneath the sun[3]
—where there is naught but pain, trouble, and
vexation of spirit[4]—
abounding in spiritual delights?'

Why should I not speak of delights—
the grace of virginity
with the gift of fruitfulness,
the guerdon of humility,
the honeycomb which drops charity [5]
the bowels of mercy [6]
the fullness of grace
the privilege of singular glory?

The queen of the world
coming up from the wilderness then[7]
—as the Church sings [8]—
has become fair
even to the angels
and she is gentle in her delights.

Let them cease from marvelling
at the delights of this wilderness,
for the Lord has given his blessing
and our earth has brought forth its increase. [9]

Why do they marvel
that Mary goes up from the wilderness
abounding in delights?

Let them instead marvel
that Christ came down
from the richness of the heavenly kingdom
as a poor man.

For it seems a far greater miracle
that the Son of God was made
a little lower than the angels[10]
than that the Mother of God should be exalted
above the angels.

Bernard *of* Clairvaux [11]

[1] Sg 8:5
[2] Ps 45:5
[3] Si 1:14 CK
[4] Ps 89:10
[5] Sg 4:11
[6] Lk 1:78

[7] Sg 3:65
[8] Antiphon *Speciosa facta es*
[9] Ps 84:11
[10] Heb 2:9
[11] Sermon Four for the Feast of
the Assumption, 1

Let us contemplate the Lord,
clinging to the ladder,
and the angels ascending and descending
towards the Virgin.

They marvel at the pure maiden
the mother of the Lord
soon to be the queen of heaven,
and they break forth
in these words of wonder and praise:
'Who is she who ascends in pure whiteness?'[1]

What is 'pure whiteness'
if not the adornment with white vesture?

Adorned surely with the adornment
of beauty and honor
of righteousness and holiness.

Who is she
who ascends in pure whiteness?
Who is she
who goes forth as the rising dawn,
beautiful as the moon,
excellent as the sun[2]
—as we read elsewhere.

As the dawn
rising from darkness to light,
from error to faith,
from the world to God,
and in the faint gleam of her rising,
tinged with the crimson of modesty,
with the lovely pallor of humility.

Beautiful as the moon
because for ever remaining chaste,
she is bathed in the brilliance of heavenly light
and rejoices in its overshadowing.

Everywhere brilliance
everywhere splendor
everywhere
the whiteness of her garments is signified.

Of this whiteness
other things might have been said;
as that word of the Lord,
who said concerning his own:
They shall walk with me in white for they are worthy.[3]
and
*Someone who has conquered
shall be clothed in white garments.*[4]

Let us now hear about the odor of these same
garments:
the words of the bridegroom
praising the bride
in the marriage song:
The door of your garments is as the odor of incense.[5]

They say
that by the odor of incense
demons are put to flight
tears are evoked,
God is appeased
by intercessory tears.

The fragrance of Mary's garments
puts enemies to flight,
attracts the good,
and placates God.

Her head is covered
with the glory of her virginity
and veiled in the scarlet of charity.
The blessing of the Lord is upon it
and it is filled with the blessings of all nations.[6]
It is crowned with the crowns of all peoples
and goes forth to the rejoicing of all.

See in the beauty of her diadem
the assembling of saints
exulting in her quivering and reflecting light.

That crown is
red with roses,
white with lilies,
pale with violets,
green with laurels,
heavy with palms,
rich in oil,
filled with every fruit,
packed with every sweetness.

By her holy leading
we should be prepared to treat of deeper matters
and more secret mysteries
leading us to the vision of God.

Amadeus *of* Lausanne [7]

[1] Sg 3:6
[2] Sg 6:9
[3] Rev 3:4
[4] Rev 3:5
[5] Sg 4:11
[6] Gen 27:29
[7] Second Homily on the Praises of Blessed Mary

Notice

with what prayers
we could have led you
and have followed you from afar
in rising up to your Son,
O blessed Virgin.

May it be of your loving-kindness
to make known to the world
that grace
which you found with God,
by obtaining by your prayers
pardon for the guilty
healing for the sick
strength for the fainthearted
consolation for the afflicted
help for those in danger
and
freedom for your saints.

On this day of solemnity and joy,
gracious Queen,
may your Son our Lord
shower the gifts of his grace
on your servants
who call with praise
upon the utterly sweet name of Mary,
for he is God
above all
blessed throughout all ages.
Amen.

Bernard *of* Clairvaux [1]

[1] Fourth Sermon for the Feast of the Assumption, 9

The New Eve

D eath reigned from Adam to Moses, even over those whose sins were not like the transgression of Adam, who was a type of the one who was to come.

Romans 5:14

As by a man came death, by a man has come also the resurrection of the dead. For as in Adam all die, so also in Christ shall all be made alive. But each in his own order: Christ the first fruits, then at his coming those who belong to Christ.

1 Corinthians 15:22-23

Adam was formed first, then Eve; and Adam was not deceived, but the woman was deceived and became a transgressor. Yet woman will be saved through bearing children, if she continues in faith and love and holiness, with modesty.

1 Timothy 2: 13-15

One man and one woman
did us grievous harm,
yet nevertheless
—thanks be to God—
by
one man and one woman.

The gift
is not proportionate to the loss
but the amplitude of mercy
exceeds the value
of the benefits lost.[1]

Just as a prudent and careful workman
does not destroy but remakes
what is spoiled[2]
in a much more useful form,
so for our sake
He made the new Adam from the old,
and transmuted Eve into Mary.

While Christ was able to be sufficient for us,
and now all our sufficiency is of him,[3]
it was not good for us
that the man should be alone.[4]

It was more appropriate
that each sex take part
in our restoration
since both took part
in its downfall.

Clearly
that man Christ Jesus
is the faithful and powerful
Mediator between God and man[5]
but people stand in awe of his divine majesty.

His humanity
seems to be absorbed
in his divinity,
not because its substance is changed,
but because his disposition[6] is deified

We hymn
not only his mercy
but also his judgement
because
even if he learned compassion
from the things that he suffered[7]
and so is merciful,
even so,
he also has the power of judgement.[8]

In short,
our God is a consuming fire.[9]
How can a sinner not shrink at coming near,
for fear of perishing in the sight of God
as wax melts when exposed to fire.[10]

So the woman
who is blessed among women[11]
will be seen to be not purposeless;
in this reconciliation;
a place will be found for her.

For we need a mediator with our Mediator
and for us there is no one better suited
than Mary.

Eve
—through whom the old serpent
poured out his poisonous venom
on humankind[12]—
is a very callous mediatrix;

Mary
—who provided the antidote of salvation
to men and to women—
is a trustworthy mediatrix.

The one was a handmaid of seduction;
the other of propitiation.

The one wrought lies
the other brought redemption.

Why does human frailty tremble
before Mary?

In her
there is nothing stern
nothing terrifying.

She is utterly gentle
offering milk and wool to all.[13]

Turn over carefully in your mind
the whole course of sacred history
and note
whether in Mary
there is any chiding,
any harshness,
or any sign of even the slightest anger,
let alone anything to cause you to be wary
or to shrink form approaching her.

But if you find that she is instead
full of every kind of loving-kindness and grace
full of gentleness and mercy
—as indeed she is—
then give thanks to Him
who of his ever-tender mercy foresaw
your need of such a mediatrix.

In short,
she became all things to all people[14]
and of her utterly bountiful charity
she made herself debtor to all
both wise and foolish.[15]

She opened to everyone
her lap of mercy,
that everyone might receive
of her fullness:[16]
the captive might find redemption
the sick, healing
the sad, consolation
the sinner, pardon
the just, grace
the angel, joy
not least
the Holy Trinity, glory
and the person of the Son,
the substance of human flesh,
so that no one should be hidden
from her warmth.[17]

Bernard *of* Clairvaux

[1] Rm 5:15
[2] Mt 12:20
[3] 2 Cor 3:5
[4] Gen 23:18
[5] 1 Tm 2:5
[6] *Affectio*, affection, in Latin
[7] Heb 5:8
[8] Heb 2:17
[9] Heb 12:29
[10] Ps 67:3
[11] Lk 1:28
[12] Gen 3:6
[13] Cf. Is 1:18
[14] 1 Cor 9:22
[15] Rom 1:14
[16] Cf Jn 1:16
[17] Cf. Ps 18:7
[18] Sermon for the Octave of the Assumption, 1-2

We need to distinguish
two sorts of greeting
because there are two distinct sorts of salvation.

There is a vain salvation:
of which it is written,
Vain in the salvation of man[1]

And there is a true salvation:
of which it is written,
Hear me in the truth of your salvation.[2]

But the angelic greeting
[to Mary]
whether a yearning prayer
for a salvation much desired
or the proclamation
of salvation given and received,
does not proffer false friendship
on the part of him who gives the greeting,
nor does it proclaim false praise of the Virgin.

For just as virginity
is always dear to the angels,
so the praises [the angel] utters of the Virgin
are truly sincere,
and he begins
by praising her fullness of grace, saying
Hail, full of grace.

O saving greeting,
spoken by the angel,
instructing us in how we should greet the Virgin.

O joy of the heart,
sweetness to the mouth,
seasoning of love!

Where there is fullness of grace
what place can there be for anger?

For fullness of grace
renders the first sin void
and restores nature.

Sin
it was
which corrupted nature
and gave rise to anger

But God, in his anger,
has not suppressed his mercies.

He has poured out grace
and turned away his anger.

That sex
which he condemned and cursed
in the first woman,
he now
in the blessed Virgin,
fills with the grace of his blessing
and the oil of his mercy.

This is the cruse of oil,[3]
this is the vessel of Gideon filled with dew,[4]
this is the golden jar
containing the manna of surpassing sweetness
which rained down from heaven.[5]

Who can conceive
the nature and the abundance
of the grace which filled her
who is named first among women,
who alone is called
full of grace,
who gave birth to the only-begotten Son,
full of grace and truth?

Baldwin *of* Forde [6]

[1] Ps 59:13 [60:12]
[2] Ps 68:14 [69:13]
[3] 1 Kg 17:12
[4] Jg 6:38
[5] Heb 9:4
[6] Tractate 7

Eve,
run to Mary.
Run to your daughter.

Let your daughter now plead
for her mother
and take away
the mother's reproach.

Let her now reconcile
her mother
with her Father.

For if man fell
on account of a woman
surely he will rise
only through another woman.

What was it you said, Adam?
The woman
whom you gave me
to be with me,
she gave me the fruit of the tree
and I ate. [1]

What evil words!
Far from excusing you
they condemn you. [2]

Wisdom
however
prevails against evil.

The occasion for pardon
which God endeavored to draw from you
by his cross-examination
—but could not—
he found in the treasure
of his never failing kindness. [3]

He gave
woman for woman
a wise
for a foolish [4]
a humble
for an arrogant. [5]

Instead of the tree of death
she offers you
a taste of life.

In place of the poisonous fruit of bitterness
she holds out to you
the sweetness of eternity's fruit.

Change your words
of evil excuse
into a song of thanksgiving
and say:

'Lord,
the woman whom you have given to be with me
she gave me the fruit of the tree of life
and I ate.
And it was sweeter than honey to my mouth [6]
for by it
you have given me life.'

For this
was the angel
sent to the Virgin.

O Virgin maid,
admirable
and worthy of all our honor. [7]

O uniquely venerable woman!
O fairest among all women!

You have repaired your parents' weakness
and restored
life
to all their offspring.

Bernard *of* Clairvaux [8]

[1] Gen 3:12
[2] Cf Wis 17:11
[3] Cf Sir 30:23
[4] Cf Mt 25:2

[5] Cf. 1 Cor 5:2
[6] Ps 119:103
[7] Sg 7:6
[8] Homily Two in Praise of the Blessed Virgin Mary, 3

How pure and radiant was that flesh,
brought forth by the virgin,
conceived by the Holy Spirit.

The glory of his holiness was inherited from his
mother
as well as from the Holy Spirit,
and so it was inviolable in itself,
besides giving health to the whole stock.

In the past, a foolish woman,
Eve,
poured the leaven of concupiscence
into the mass of human nature,
and by that very act
made this leaven
an hereditary and inescapable necessity.

So likewise,
through some new and miraculously unchanged law,
the wisest of virgins
poured straight into her son
—as his natural inheritance—
the leaven of innocence and sanctity,
by the wisdom and power of the Holy Spirit.

If blessed Job could say
that compassion took root in him
from the beginning
and piety issued forth from his mother's womb;[1]
and if the apostle maintained
that Timothy had to some extent
inherited the grace of faith,
first from his grandmother Lois
and then from his mother Eunice:[2]
then how much more
is that which was born of the spotless flesh
of the virgin
through the working of the Holy Spirit,
unable to be anything
but virginal and free from all corruption.

The disease of original sin
was not able wholly to infect and poison
human nature.

It stops short
at destroying in the bodies of newborn infants
the tiny flower of virginity,
though frail indeed and weak.

In actuality, everyone,
even if conceived in sin,
is born a virgin.
How much more then
does virginal conception
followed by virginal childbirth
make hereditary the splendor of holiness!

This is not the inheritance of corruptible innocence
—that we spoke of above—
but an unfading inheritance of angelic purity.

Let me add that if
—by the kindness of our creator—
that original mark
was so deeply imprinted in our first parents
that it was too strong to be uprooted
from deep in the flesh
by any subsequent appearance of sons or grandsons
—whether of their own parentage or,
afterwards, of others—
to a far greater extend
the virgin Mary had the power
to pass on an inheritance to her child!

We believe that
in her
through the overshadowing power of the most High,
human nature flowered again to spotless innocence.

I am not saying
that in her the heat of bodily concupiscence
was tamed and lulled to rest.

I am saying
that to her very depths
it was killed and buried,
so that the glory of virginal honor,
which she herself received as a free gift,
she transmitted by heredity to her offspring.

There is this point too.
All christian piety
—without any agitation or disagreement—
is of the one opinion:
that if the first stock of our race had remained pure,
original justice and inviolable innocence
would have descended to their posterity
by the law of inheritance.

Why then should she
—who once more renewed the ancient privilege
yes, and in a far more excellent manner—
why should she be deprived of
at least the normal privilege,
as it should have been?

Mohn of Ford [3]

[1] Cf Jb 31:18
[2] Cf 2 Tim 1:5
[3] Sermon 8 on the Song of Songs, 4

Today

is the birthday of the new Mother
who has destroyed the curse brought
by the first mother
so that all those who
through the fault of the first
had been born under the yoke
of eternal condemnation
through her
might instead inherit a blessing.

She is truly the new mother
for she has brought new life to her children
—already hardening with age—
and has healed the defect
of both inborn and acquired senility.

Indeed yes.
She is the new mother
who by an unheard of miracle
has given birth in such a way that
becoming a mother
she has not ceased to be a virgin.

And she has given birth to the Child
who created all things,
even the mother herself.

Guerric of Igny [1]

[1] Sermon 51.1: for the Feast of the Nativity of Mary

God is the author of all benefits,
but after him,
praise is due first to the Virgin,
who deserves to be blessed by all.

For this reason
the angel said to her
Blessed are you among women,
as also Elizabeth said
Blessed are you among women.[1]

Eve,
through pride
and the sign of disobedience,
brought down on herself a curse,
and through her we are subject to this curse.

Pride deserves a curse
for God resists the proud
but gives grace to the humble. [2]

This is why it is written
Pride is the beginning of all sin.
Whoever clings to it will be filled with curses.[3]

Mary
however
humbled herself
and deserved a blessing.

Baldwin *of* Forde [4]

[1] Lk 1:28, 42
[2] 1 P 5:5
[3] Si 10:35
[4] Tractate 7

O virgin maid

admirable and worthy of all honor.[1]
O uniquely venerable woman!
O fairest among all women.[2]
You have repaired your parents' weakness
and restored life to all their offspring.[3]

Bernard of Clairvaux [4]

---

[1] Cf Sg 7:6
[2] Sg 5:9
[3] Cf Ruth 4:15
[4] Homily Two in Praise of the Blessed Virgin Mary, 3

On the sixth day
of the first age
our nature was made
in the image and likeness of God.[1]

In the sixth epoch of the world[2]
God came to be
in the image and likeness
of our nature.

In the first instance
man came from earth;
in the latter
God came from Mary.

At the first
man came
—upright and undefiled—
from still untainted and virgin earth.

At this latest
the just God and Creator of virgins
comes from the ever-untainted Virgin Mary.

There
woman was created from the side of man
without a mother;
here
Man is begotten from a woman's womb
without a father.

There
woman is formed
from the rib of sleeping Adam
to be his helpmate[3];
here
the bride is consecrated
from the side of the Christ who died.

 Isaac of Stella [4]

[1] Gn 1:26
[2] See Isaac's sermons 42 and 43
[3] Cf. Gn 2:18, 21-22
[4] Sermon 54.7: for the Feast of the Nativity of Mary.

The fruitfulness of Mary
benefits us
in three ways.

It turns away the yoke of our ancient captivity.
It turns aside the wrath of divine indignation.
And it effaces the mark of human iniquity.

Bernard *of* Clairvaux [1]

[1] Sentences, 2.58

The Woman Clothed with the Sun

A great portent appeared in heaven: a woman clothed with the sun, with the moon under her feet, and on her head a crown of twelve stars. She was pregnant and was crying out in birthpangs, in the agony of giving birth. Then another portent appeared in heaven : a great red dragon, with seven heads and ten horns, and seven diadems on his heads. His tail swept down a third of the starts of heaven and threw them to the earth. Then the dragon stood before the woman who was about to bear a child, so that he might devour her child as soon as it was born. And she gave birth to a son, a male child, who is to rule all the nations with a rod of iron. But her child was snatched away and taken to God and to this throne, and the woman fled into the wilderness, where she has a place prepared by God. . . .

Revelation 12:1-6

Do you think that

Mary is the woman clothed with the sun?[1]

Let it be so,
inasmuch as the very connection may show that
this is what the Church understands
by this prophetic vision.

But it may clearly be seen
that this cannot inappropriately
be attributed to Mary.
Surely it is she who put on herself
another sun.

As it rises on the good and bad alike[2]
so she too does not disregard past deserts
but shows herself approachable to the entries of all
and generously accepting of all.
And she pities the needs of all
with the amplest tenderness.

For every shortcoming is beneath her
and whatever the fragility or corruption
she overcomes it;
with a far more wonderful excellence
she excels all creatures,
so that the moon may deservedly be said
to be beneath her feet.

In other respects
it seems that we have said nothing strange
in saying that the moon was beneath her feet,
we cannot doubt that she is exalted
above all the angel choirs [3]
above Cherubim and Seraphim.

The moon, however, designates
not only the shortcomings
but also the foolishness
of the mind
—and sometimes of the Church of this age—
first
because of its changeableness
and then
because it takes its splendor from elsewhere.

In both cases
—as I shall point out—
the moon
may properly be understood to be
beneath Mary's feet
in one way or another:
for the fool changes like the moon,
but the wise remains constant like the sun. [4]

In the sun
is intense heat and abiding splendor;
in the moon,
splendor alone
and it is altogether changeable and uncertain [5]
never staying in one phase.

Justly then is Mary said to be
clothed in the sun:
she has penetrated the profoundest depths of divine
wisdom
—even beyond what can be believed;
as far as her condition as a created being allows
without personal union
she seems to be bathed in that light inaccessible.[6]

By that intense fire
are the lips of the prophets cleansed
and by that fire
do the Seraphim blaze.

Mary
—far differently—
deserved not merely to be touched,
but to be covered
to be embraced
—and as it were–
to be enclosed
by fire.

So may we regard
the glistering
—yes, and the blistering—[7]
clothing of this woman,
whose every quality shines so brightly
that there can be no hint
—I say not—
of any darkness
but not even of any dimness
or faint light,
no lukewarmness
no anything
save utterly luminous brightness.

Bernard *of* Clairvaux [8]

[1] Rev 12:1
[2] Mt 5:25
[3] *Exaltata est sancta Dei Genitrix*: an antiphon used on the Feast of the Assumption.
[4] Si 27:12
[5] Jb 14:2
[6] 1 Tm 6:16
[7] *candidissmus...calidissimus*, literally, whitest...hottest
[8] Sermon for the Octave of the Assumption, 3

A woman clothed with the sun,
Scripture says,
with the moon under her feet.[1]

Let us caress the footmarks of Mary,
my brothers,
and with devoted supplication
let us trace her blessed steps.

Let us hold her[2]
and not let go of her
until she blesses us, [3]
for she has power.[4]

Surely
she is the fleece set between the dew
and the threshing floor.[5]
the woman between the sun and the moon,
Mary between Christ and the Church.

Yet perhaps you marvel
more at the woman clothed with the sun
than at the fleece covered with dew?

Between the sun and the woman
there is similarity
and a marvelous kinship.

How does so frail a nature exist
in such blazing heat?
Deservedly do you marvel,
blessed Moses,
and with great curiosity you yearn
to look more closely.

Put off the shoes from your feet[6] indeed
and put a veil over your worldly thoughts,
if you long to approach.

I am going, he says,
I am going to look at this great sight. [7]

Clearly a great sight:
a bush burning yet unconsumed,[8]
a great sign:
a woman clothed with the sun
yet unscathed.

It is not within the nature of a shrub
to be covered in flames
and still remain unconsumed;
it is not within the power of a woman
to endure being clothed with the sun.
It is not within human power
—no, nor angelic;
it requires a much higher power.

The Holy Spirit
he says
will come upon you.

And she replied, as it were:
God is a spirit [9]
and *our God is a consuming fire.*[10]

The power of the Most High,
he says,
not mine, nor yours,
will overshadow you.[11]

There is nothing amazing
that, being thus overshadowed,
she could endure being thus clothed.

Bernard *of* Clairvaux [12]

[1] Rev 12:1
[2] Sg 3:4
[3] Gen 32:26
[4] Rom 11:23
[5] Jdg 6:36-46
[6] Ex 3:6
[7] Ex 3:3
[8] Ex 3:2
[9] Jn 4:24
[10] Heb 12:29
[11] Lk 1:35
[12] Sermon for the Octave of the Assumption, 5

On her head
say the Scriptures
is a crown of twelve stars.[1]

Worthy indeed
was her head
to be crowned with stars
since it shone far brighter than they.
She adorned them
rather than they adorning her.

Why should stars not crown her
who is clad in the sun?...

According to our limitations
avoiding the danger of probing secret matters,
we may understand
by those twelve stars with which
Mary is singularly adorned
twelve special privileges.

In Mary
may be found
the privilege of heaven
the privilege of the flesh
the privilege of the heart.

And if these three were multiplied by four
we should have the twelve stars
with which our queen's crown glistens.

For me certainly
the brilliance flashes
first in the birth of Mary
second in angel's greeting
third in the Spirit's overshadowing
fourth in the unutterable conception
of the Son of God.

Likewise
the brightness of the stars
shines forth with glory in these too:
the archetype of virginity
fecundity without corruption
pregnancy without weariness
childbearing without pain.

No less in Mary
does the gentleness of modesty
shine particularly forth
and the devotion of humility
the generosity of belief
and the martyrdom of the heart.

Bernard *of* Clairvaux [2]

---

[1] Sg 3:11
[2] Sermon for the Octave of the Assumption, 7

Full of Grace

And the angel came to her and said,
'Hail, full of grace, the Lord is with you!'

Luke 1:28

Fear not, Mary,
you have found grace with the Lord.[1]

How much grace?

Full grace
unique grace.

Unique or general?
Both surely.
Because full,
both unique and general.

You have received the general grace uniquely.
Both unique and general, I say,
for you alone found grace above everyone.

Unique
for you along found it in its fullness.

General
for from that fullness all may receive it.

Blessed are you among women
and blessed is the fruit of your womb.[2]

Uniquely of your womb is the fruit,
but it comes to the being of all
through you.

Bernard *of* Clairvaux [3]

[1] Cf Lk 1:30 and the Annunciation antiphon *Ne timeas*
[2] Lk 1:42
[3] Sermon Three for the Annunciation, 8 .

Page 273

God
the author of miracles
worked three specific wonders
in Mary.

He marvelously instilled
full purity in her
so that the ark of the covenant could be covered
with the purest gold.[1]

He made her virginal purity
flourish powerfully
so that the burning bush could not be consumed.[2]

He remarkably joined together
the lowest things with the highest,
so that through the medium of Jacob's ladder[3]
earthly things could be linked
with heavenly ones.

Bernard *of* Clairvaux [4]

[1] Cf Ex 25:11
[2] Cf Ex 3:2
[3] Gen 28:12
[4] Sentences, series 2.57

Clearly that womb was blessed
even before it carried the Lord

ᛒ

Day and night
with the purest desire
and the longing of a holy and consecrated love
it prepared itself to bear its holy burden.

In the silence of her heart
Mary said to herself
Let him kiss me with the kiss of his mouth.[1]

There has never been another soul
or rather,
there has never been one of the blessed spirits
—not even from the most blissful
of the nine choirs—
that takes its name from the fire of charity
and refreshes the heat of its immense love
by the continual contemplation of eternity
and the ceaseless praise of the holy Trinity;
no, not even among the cherubim
has there been anyone
who made progress like hers
in desiring and receiving this kiss.

To make her ready
for such great grace
from her mother's womb she was fashioned[2]
by him who *establishes the heavens*[3]
and every single moment
during the successive stages
by which God *established* her
the fullness of grace was built up.

One day she would become
God's mother
and then an angel would call her
full of grace.

So her womb is blessed
in the very manner of its establishment
in blessedness
yet it is far more blessed when it
finally
in a divine and indescribable way
receives its most blessed burden.

Blessed indeed
yes, utterly blessed,
is that womb
when it bore him
when it formed him
when it was in labor with him
when it brought him to birth.

John *of* Ford [4]

[1] Sg 1:1
[2] Cf Ps 139:13
[3] Cf Jb 28:27
[4] Sermon 70 on the Song of Songs, 4

Life eternal

is
a never-failing fountain
which waters the whole surface of paradise.
Not only waters it
but saturates it.

A garden fountain
a well of living waters
flowing, surging.[1]

And who is the fount of life
but Christ our Lord?

This heavenly stream came down
through a channel[2]
concealing the full measure of the fount
yet letting droplets of grace fall
on our thirsty hearts
more to one
to another less.

The channel is full, surely,
that others may receive
of its fullness
yet not the fullness itself.

You have guessed
—I am sure—
whom I mean by this channel
who
taking its fullness
from the heart of the Father himself
has poured it out on us
—not as it is
but as we are capable of receiving it.

You are aware
to whom was said
Hail, full of grace.[3]

Do we find it astounding
that someone could be found
from whom
so great and wonderful a channel could come,
whose highest point
—like the ladder which the patriarch Jacob saw—
could touch the heavens
and indeed pass beyond the heavens
and reach the fountain
the living waters
which are beyond the heavens?

℔

But how did this our channel
reach so sublime a fount?

How do you suppose,
if not by intense desire,
if not by fervent devotion
if not by pure prayer?

As it is written:
The prayer of the righteous pierces the heavens.[4]

And who is this just person
if not Mary the Just
from whom the Sun of Justice
rose for us.

How did she reach
the inaccessible heights of majesty
if not by
knocking
asking
seeking?

At last she found what she sought:
she to whom it was said:
You have found favor with God.[5]

What?
She is full of grace
and yet she still finds grace?

She is truly worthy
to find what she seeks.
Her own fullness was not enough
she could not rest content with her own goodness
—but as it is written—
Whoever drinks me, will still thirst[6] —
she pleads for overflowing grace
for the salvation of the universe.

The Holy Spirit will come upon you[7]
Scripture says
and that precious ointment shall flow over you
so abundantly and so copiously
that it will overflow abundantly in every direction.

So it is:
now we sense it
our faces are shining with oil
Now we cry out:
your name is as ointment poured forth
your name is remembered from generation to generation.[8]

Bernard of Clairvaux [9]

[1] Sg 4:15
[2] Literally, an aqueduct, a water-channel
[3] Lk 1:28
[4] Cf Si 35:21
[5] Lk 1:28
[6] Si 24:29
[7] Lk 1:35
[8] Sg 1:2
[9] Third Homily for the Feast of the Nativity of Mary, 4

Let us gaze
upon her glory
and, entering the depth of so great a light,
with swelling heart and unspeakable joy
let us hasten
through the vivid brightness of the paths,
saying with Solomon,
Her paths are lovely
and all her ways are peaceful.[1]

First of all,
she was deemed worthy
to be adorned
with the beauty of all the virtues.

Secondly,
she was united to the Holy Spirit
in a bond of wedlock.

Thirdly,
she was found the Mother of the Saviour.

Fourthly,
a sword pierced her soul
and by the flesh taken of her flesh
the ruin of the lost world
is restored.

Fifthly,
she rejoices in her Son
arising and ascending
above the heaven of heavens
to the right hand of the Father.

Sixthly,
she is caught up from this world
and as the Lord hastens to meet her
she is placed above the denizens of heaven.

Seventhly,
she will be completed
when the fulness of the Gentiles shall have entered
and all Israel shall be saved. [2]

For beyond what is appropriately said or believed,
she rejoices
in the general salvation of the elect,
knowing that it was for them
that the Son of God
took flesh from her.

Then, therefore,
will she be fulfilled,
God providing a better thing,
lest without us
she should not be made perfect.[3]

Amadeus of Lausanne [4]

[1] Pr 3:17
[2] Rom 11:25-26
[3] Heb 11:40
[4] Homily Two on the Praises of Blessed Mary

She was cleansed of blood. [1]

In this passage,
the stain of original sin
is indicated through the image of blood.

The divine mercy
banished it from the blessed Virgin
so that it remained in her
in terms of
neither act nor guilt.

The Son of God so sanctified his tabernacle
that no inclinations to lust remained in her,
no inducements to vice.

For he who stopped the flow of blood
from the woman with a hemorrhage
through a merely touch of his robe[2]
kept from his mother
all stain of original sin.

 Bernard *of* Clairvaux [3]

[1] Ezk 16:9
[2] Mt 9:20-22
[3] Sentences, series 3.111

I have gathered my myrrh with my spices[1]
he says.
Immortality and incorruptibility indeed
he gathered after death.

ß

In Jesus
there is neither corruption
nor its cause.

In his Mother
though there be its cause
still there is no corruption.

In all others
there is both corruption and its cause.

Our myrrh
represses the rising of movements of carnal
concupiscence.

Mary's myrrh
knew nothing of such movements.

Jesus' myrrh
had neither the cause nor the beginning
of being so moved.

Of his fullness
we have all received[2]
and myrrh from his myrrh.

The myrrh of our chastity
is from the gift and the imitation of himself.

Therefore
when he harvests myrrh in us
he is harvesting his own myrrh.

May he find much myrrh in me to harvest.

Gilbert *of* Hoyland [3]

---

[1] Song of Songs 5:1
[2] Jn 1:10
[3] Sermon 40 on the Song of Songs, 6

The integrity of the Virgin
and the chastity of her mind and body
were such that she was
wholly virgin
wholly undefiled
wholly unstained
in none of her senses corrupt
in none of her senses impure.

She blushed at all things shameful.
She condemned all things wicked.
She desired all things seemly.
She abominated all things dishonorable.

The perfection of virginity
is the inviolate integrity
of all one's senses,
and every detraction from this integrity
is a sort of deflowering of virginity.

This is the radiant color
—the whiteness of chastity
combined with the rosiness of modesty—
which shines on the face of the Virgin
and adds to the grace of her beauty.

She was therefore so radiantly colored
with chastity
as well as modesty,
that in her was realized
that which is written:
A holy and chaste woman has a double beauty.[1]

Full of grace.
Her cheerful expression further added to her grace,
and her face was gladdened
with the oil of exultation.[2]

With total devotion
and the full fervor of charity,
she offered herself to God
in an odor of sweetness.

More than all the daughters of Sion
who rejoice in their king,[3]
her spirit rejoiced
in God her Saviour.[4]

See the beauty of her face:
how the grace of regularity formed it
how the grace of whiteness and rosiness illumined it
how the grace of cheerfulness gladdened it.

Yet not only is her face beautiful,
but she is wholly beautiful,
and he who found in her his joy
bears witness to this when he says,
You are wholly beautiful, my love,
and in you there is no stain.[5]

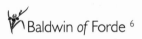Baldwin *of* Forde [6]

[1] Cf Sir 26:9
[2] Heb 1:9
[3] Cf Ps 149:2
[4] Lk 1:47
[5] Sg 4:7
[6] Tractate 7

To imagine that a privilege
which has been accorded to some mortals,
albeit few,
was denied to that virgin
through whom all mortals have entered life
would be intolerable.

Beyond all doubt
the Mother of the Lord
was holy
before she was born.

I think that there came upon her
a yet more ample blessing of sanctification
which not only sanctified her birth,
but kept her life thereafter immune from sin
something which is believed to have been accorded
to no other born of woman.

This unique privilege of sanctity
whereby she was enabled to live her whole life
without sin
is surely appropriate
for the Queen of virgins
who
—in giving birth to him
who destroyed sin and death—
obtained for all the reward of life and justice.

Her birth was holy, then,
because great sanctity from the womb made it holy.

Bernard *of* Clairvaux[1]

[1] Letter 174.3

The living and active word of God
cuts more keenly than any two-edged sword.[1]
Of it Our Saviour said:
*I have not come to send peace
but the sword.*[2]

A polished arrow[3] too
is that special love of Christ
which not only pierced Mary's soul
but penetrated through and through,[4]
until the tiniest space in her virginal breast
was permeated by love.

Thenceforth she would love
with her whole heart
her whole soul
and her whole strength[5]
and be full of grace.[6]

It trans-pierced her thus
that it might come down
even to us
and of that fullness
we might all receive.[7]

She would become the mother of that love
whose father is the God who is love.[8]

And when that love was brought to birth
he would place his tent in the sun[9]
that the Scripture might be fulfilled:
I will make you the Light of the Nations
that you may be my salvation
to the ends of the earth.[10]

This was fulfilled
through Mary
who brought forth in visible flesh
him
whom she conceived invisibly
neither from the flesh
nor by means of the flesh.

In the process
she experienced through her whole being
a wound of love
that was mighty and sweet.

And I would reckon myself happy if
–at rare moments–
I felt at least the prick of the point of that sword.

Even if bearing only love's slightest wound
I could still say:
I am wounded with love.[11]

Bernard *of* Clairvaux[12]

[1] Heb 4:12

[2] Mt 10:34

[3] Is 49:2

[4] Cf Lk 2:35

[5] Cf Mk 12:30

[6] Cf Lk 1:28

[7] Cf Jn 1:16

[8] 1 Jn 4:8

[9] Ps 18:6

[10] Is 49:6

[11] Sg 2:5 LXX

[12] Sermon 29 on the Song of Songs, 8

Having been made the agent and collaborator
in the divine plan
she gave us the salvation of the world
for she brought forth
for us
the Saviour
who is himself the world's salvation.

She could not, however, do this alone
and therefore
she offered her service
revealed her role as mediator
and brought forth in our midst
the Mediator
who could indeed bring it about.

And it was for this reason that she was rightly told
The Lord is with you.

You are to effect a sublime work.
Through you
the salvation of the world is to be achieved
and the rod of the oppressor is to be broken
as it was in the day of Midian.[1]

That for which you have been chosen
surpasses all human power and wisdom
but the Lord is with you
and for him
nothing is impossible[2].

In the work of our salvation
—which begins from fullness of grace
and is consummated in fulness of grace—
fullness of grace
is specifically mentioned
and praise is ascribed to the Author of grace
who with the cooperation of the Virgin
is revealed as the author of this work.

Baldwin *of* Forde [3]

[1] Is 9:4
[2] Lk 1:37
[3] Tractate 7

Mary says:
*This is my beloved
and this is my Son,
O daughters of Jerusalem*[1]

'He is the *blessed fruit of* my *womb*[2]
the fruit of my flowers produced.'

She does not say
'my flower'
but 'my flowers'
for though she is a holy virgin
the flower of virginity in her
is multiform.

In her
by a singular privilege
it grows in greater profusion
than in anyone else.
She who was wholly beautiful
within and without
was bedecked with the perfect fullness
of the blossoms and loveliness
of virginity.

In you too
chastity reaches perfection.
Not only will the bloom of it show in your body
but a certain divine holiness will take possession
of your whole being.

There will be no petulant or wandering gaze
but a demeanor radiant with modesty;
no suggestive or improper talk
but speech pleasantly diffident
or seasoned with wisdom.

There will be no itching ears
eager to listen to faddish ideas or filthy stories
nor will the palate ever be desirous of tasty morsels.

The gait will be not hurried
but reserved;
dress will not be
—I will not say immodest—
it will not be unbecoming.
Instead it will be in perfect accord
with the life of religion.

The whole person will be so alive
with the grace of your holy way of living
that you will be able to say
—when you invite the Bridegroom
into your chamber—
Our bed is strewn with flowers.[3]

Guerric of Igny [4]

[1] Cf Sg 5:16
[2] Cf Lk 1:42
[3] Sg 1:15
[4] Sermon 51.5, on the Feast of the Nativity of Mary

Every holy and reasonable soul,[1]
examining the secret mysteries of heaven
and marking out the rank of heavenly spirit,
finds first
after the Redeemer
the woman blessed among women,
full of grace,[2]
the one who brought forth God
yet did not lose the glory of her virginity.

This blessed Virgin,
more brilliant than every light,
more pleasing than every sweetness,
more eminent than every dominion,
lights up the whole world and,
renewing all things
by the pouring forth of her precious ointment,[3]
surpasses the ranks of cherubim and seraphim
both in power and majesty.

Therefore let the King,
through her glorious merits,
admit us to his chamber;[4]
and David's offspring
—who shuts and no one opens[5]—
will disclose to us his hidden secrets.

He opens and no one closes.
Let him reveal to us
the joys of her who bore him,
the beauty of his chosen Mother.

Amadeus *of* Lausanne [6]

[1] Cf. Rm 12:1
[2] Lk 1:28
[3] Is 39:2, cf. Am 6:6
[4] Sg 1:3, 2:4
[5] Rev 3:7; Magnificat antiphon for 20 December
[6] Homily One on the Praises of Blessed Mary

The king made a great ivory throne
and overlaid it with the finest gold.[1]
If anyone wants to interpret
that great throne
which Solomon made of ivory
as the very body
which our Peacemaker
took today from the Virgin
he would not seem to be far from the truth. . .

For my part
I prefer to wonder
at that ivory of virginal chastity
so precious
—or rather priceless—
of which He who sits above the cherubim[2]
chose to make a seat for himself,
saying:
This is my resting place for ever and ever
Here will I sit
for I have chosen it.[3]

13

Mary is
whiter than snow
more ruddy than old ivory.[4]

Chastity
conferred on her, as we know,
an incomparable whiteness and charity
—or indeed martyrdom—
a ruddiness
brighter than that of all the elect of old.

For her own soul
was pierced by a sword[5]
so that the Mother
of the supreme Virgin and Martyr
might herself also be a virgin and martyr
white and ruddy
just as her Beloved is white an ruddy.[6]

Finally,
just as Solomon had nothing
among all his treasures and vast wealth
so precious
that he judged it preferable to ivory
for that magnificent work of art
the throne of his glory;
so Mary
found before the Lord
a grace all her own
above that of all of the elect
angels and men
the grace
to conceive and bear God's Son
and to have a throne of glory
carved from the ivory of her body
by the power of the Most High[7]
without the labor of hands.

13

How blessed
is that womb of ivory
from which the Redeemer's flesh of ivory was taken[8]
the price of souls
the wonder of angels
the seat of supreme majesty
and the throne of power
the food of immortal life
the medicine of sin
the restoration of health.

All those who touched him were healed of their infirmities
—we read—
*for power went out from him
and healed everyone.*[9]

Blessed is the womb that bore you[10]
Lord Jesus.

Happy is the chastity of the virginal womb
which provided the material
for this work of art.

Happy indeed,
my brothers,
is the brilliance of that ivory
—that is, the whiteness of chastity—
in preference to which
our Solomon chooses
neither the gold of worldly wisdom
nor the silver of eloquence
nor again the gem of any outstanding grace
provided that chastity is commenced
by humility
for the Lord
has looked upon the humility of his handmaid.[11]

Guerric of Igny [12]

[1] 1 Kgs 10:18
[2] Ps 98:2
[3] Ps 131:14
[4] Cf. Lam 4:7
[5] Cf Lk 2:35
[6] Cf Sg 5:10
[7] Lk 1:35
[8] Cf Lk 11:2, Sg 5:14
[9] Mt 6:56, Lk 6:18f.
[10] Lk 11:27
[11] Lk 1:48
[12] Sermon 26.3-5: First Sermon for the Feast of the Annunciation

The Virgin of virgins
herself is seen in springtime
among the flowers

and delighting in the sweetness of the fruits
and like the tree planted in the midst of paradise,[1]
she raises her head to the height of heaven

and conceiving by the heavenly dew,
brings forth
the fruit of salvation,
the fruit of glory,
the fruit of life.
And the person who eats of it
will live forever.

In one place
we read
that Christ shall be born of a virgin[2]
will suffer in the flesh
will rise again in glory
will ascend in triumph[3]
will sit at the right hand of the Father
and will bestow the gifts of the Spirit
upon believers.

In another place
we read that
he was born,
suffered,
rose,
ascended
and pours the gift of the Spirit
upon his own.

So too
in the writings of truth
it was declared of holy Mary
that a virgin should conceive
and a virgin should bring forth a son
his name Emmanuel.[4]

His going forth
should be from the beginning
from the days of eternity.[5]

Him
the Virgin was worthy to conceive
she alone to bring him forth
to suckle him
amidst the prayers and ardent expectations
of the Church
as it prays and says,
Who would give me you as my brother,
sucking my mother's breasts,
that I may find you without
and kiss you,
and no one shall now despise me.[6]

You shall I find
—she says—
without
in the light
you who are the father's secret.

I shall kiss you,
being joined to you
in the partaking of your flesh and blood,
so that no longer
are we two
but one flesh.[7]

While we desire to extol her
who was
blessed among women,[8]
we praise
the blessed fruit of her womb,
and while we seek to commend the beauty of the
tree,
we keep close to the surpassing beauty
of the fruit.

Every tree is known by its fruit
and judged by its yield.[9]

As the palm is assessed
by the sweetness of the date,
the olive tree
by the richness of the olives,
the wine
by the juice of the grapes,
so the praise of the Son
enriches the Mother
and the divine birth heaps honor
upon her who bore him.

Let us therefore enter the Holy of Holies
and gaze upon the mercy seat
which has above it
two cherubim
gazing upon it
and overshadowing it
as they face each other with wings outstretched.[10]

There among other things
shines
the golden urn
enclosing hidden manna.

There is Aaron's rod
which budded.[11]

The two cherubim
mean the two Testaments
—for 'cherubim' means the fulness of knowledge—
and the fulness of knowledge
is in the Testaments.

The golden urn
is blessed Mary,
golden
by reason of the excellence of her life,
golden
through her integrity and purity,
golden
through the fulness of grace.

This urn held the hidden manna:[12]
she in her sacred womb
bore the bread of angels
which comes down from heaven
and gives life to the world.

The priestly rod
signified that same glorious one who
—descended from a priestly and royal stock—
gave birth to the King of saints,
who is a priest for ever
after the order of Melchizedek.[13]

Truly is she called a rod
for she is gracious and upright
sensitive and straight.

Gracious
through her modesty and beauty
upright
through her justice and rectitude,
sensitive
through her capacity for contemplation,
straight
through the merit of her life.

Amadeus *of* Lausanne [14]

[1] Gen 2:9, 3:3
[2] Cf. Is 7:14
[3] Ps 47:5
[4] Is 7:14
[5] Mic 5:2
[6] Sg 8:1
[7] Gen 2:24

[8] Lk 1:28
[9] Cf Lk 7:20
[10] Cf. Ex 25:17-20
[11] Heb 9:4
[12] Cf. Rev 2:17
[13] Ps 110:4, Heb 5:6, 6:20
[14] First Homily on the Praises of Blessed Mary

Everything about her is worthy of praise.
Whatever is hers alone,
whatever she shares in common [with others]
both extol her with special praise.

Even the things she has in common
she has in a unique way,
for whatever she shares with others,
she herself possesses more than all others
in a manner surpassing all excellence.

She remains unique, therefore,
even in the things in which she is not unique.

She is chaste,
she is humble,
she is sweet and kind.

And although there are others
[who have] similar virtues,
they do not [have them] in the same way,
or to the same extent.

She surpasses all
and in all things she is
the Mistress of the World
the Queen of Heaven
of men
and of angels
the Mother of God
and his daughter
his sister
and his bride
his friend
and his neighbor.

She is his mother
by her fertile virginity
daughter
by the grace of adoption
sister
by the grace of communion
bride
by the trust of betrothal
friend
by the exchange of love
neighbor
in being near to him in likeness.
She is more lovable than all,
more honorable than all,
beautiful beyond beauty,
gracious beyond grace,
glorious beyond glory.

Baldwin *of* Forde [1]

[1] Tractate 7

Clearly that womb was blessed
even before it carried the Lord

↗3

Day and night
with the purest desire
and the longing of a holy and consecrated love
it prepared itself to bear its holy burden.

In the silence of her heart
Mary said to herself
Let him kiss me with the kiss of his mouth.[1]

There has never been another soul
or rather,
there has never been one of the blessed spirits
—not even from the most blissful
of the nine choirs—
that takes its name from the fire of charity
and refreshes the heat of its immense love
by the continual contemplation of eternity
and the ceaseless praise of the holy Trinity;
no, not even among the cherubim
has there been anyone
who made progress like hers
in desiring and receiving this kiss.

To make her ready
for such great grace
from her mother's womb she was fashioned[2]
by him who *establishes the heavens*[3]
and every single moment
during the successive stages
by which God *established* her
the fullness of grace was built up.

One day she would becomes
God's mother
and then an angel would call her
full of grace.

So her womb is blessed
in the very manner of its establishment
in blessedness
yet it is far more blessed when
in a divine and indescribable way
it finally receives
its most blessed burden.

Blessed indeed
yes, utterly blessed,
is that womb
when it bore him
when it formed him
when it was in labor with him
when it brought him to birth.

John *of* Ford [4]

[1] Sg 1:1
[2] Cf Ps 139:13
[3] Cf Jb 28:27
[4] Sermon 70 on the Song of Songs, 4

Mother of Mercy

Mother of mercy, we greet you. Our life, our sweetness, and our hope, we greet you. To you do we cry, poor banished children of Eve. To you do we sigh, mourning and weeping in this vale of tears. Turn toward us, our advocate, your merciful eyes. And after this our exile, show us the blessed fruit of your womb, Jesus. O gentle, o loving, o gracious Virgin Mary.

Salve regina, mater misericordiae. Vita, dulcedo, et spes nostra, salve. Ad te clamamus, exules filii Evæ. Ad te suspiramus, gementes et flentes in hac lacrymarum valle. Eia, ergo, advocata nostra, illos tuos misericordes oculos ad nos converte. Et Jesum, benedictum fructum ventris tui, nobis post hoc exilium ostende. O clemens, o pia, o dulcis Virgo Maria.

Antiphon, *Salve Regina*

sung after the Office of Compline
in all Cistercian monasteries

Amid all the ranks of saints,
the first place
for humility
purity
and tender love
is held by the blessed virgin,
the mother of Jesus.

And in the same way
she shines out
gloriously
above all God's lovers,
for the greatness of her charity.

This is why that title of unique glory
which the Spirit of charity
in his gracious goodness
makes common to all souls
who love Jesus
has by him been bestowed
with special reason
on the one who loves him very much more:
the title 'bride of God',
and she is called God's bride and is his bride.[1]

She it is
who truly is
the mother of fair love,[2]
as the Church sings of her.

She is the teacher of the knowledge of it
the craftsman who trains us in it
its lawgiver
the go-between
who brings about love's covenant with us.

Everything in this marriage song[3]
is directed principally
to Mary,
the principal bride of Jesus.

This remains true,
whatever form the words take,
whether from the lips of the spouse to the bride,
or in her turn, of the bride to the spouse,
or something she may say when training the maidens
or from their wonder and questioning,
as these daughters of Jerusalem ponder her words.

In her own self
in fact
Mary the bride
is the highest and most distinguished model of love,
and from her overflowing fullness,
each of the maidens receives
as much as her capacity allows.[4]
Since she is *full of grace,*
it perpetually abounds within her,
a never-failing source of marvelous pleasure
as well as total richness to every spirit,
angelic and human.

This is why the woman
who saves not only men
but even those who work like beasts of burden[5]
does not consider it robbery
to adapt that tender saying of the Word of God:
If any one thirst, let him come to me an drink.[6]
And that other saying too:
Come to me, all who desire me, and eat your fill of my produce.[7]

So any soul
who longs for a holy love for the Word
should listen to her wise invitation.

He should make haste,
he should go to her,
he should come close,
he should cling.

Believe me
—or better still,
believe the Holy Spirit:
to gain the love of Jesus
there is no shorter way
than to contemplate the beauty
of this unique
incomparable
and immense charity.

John of Ford [8]

[1] Cf Sg 4:8
[2] Sir 24:24
[3] The Song of Songs
[4] Cf Eph 4:7
[5] Ps 36:6
[6] Jn 7:37
[7] Sir 24:26
[8] Sermon 70 on the Song of Songs, 2

Mary is the new mother
for she has brought new life to her children.

13

She is the new mother
who by an unheard of miracle
has given birth
in such a way that becoming a mother
she has not ceased to be a virgin.

And she has given birth to the Child
who created all things,
even the Mother herself.

It is indeed a wonderful new thing
this fruitful virginity,
but far more wonderful
is the novelty of the Child born of it.

No one
who admits that the Child is God
finds any difficulty in believing
that his mother remained a virgin.

His birth
could in no way injure the physical integrity of his
mother,
this Child who went about making even the diseased
whole.

Though she is a holy virgin,
the flower of virginity in her is multiform.

In her,
by a singular privilege,
it grows in greater profusion than in anyone else.

She who was wholly beautiful
within and without,
was bedecked with the perfect fullness of the
blossom and loveliness of virginity.

Guerric of Igny [1]

[1] Sermon 51.1: First Sermon for the Feast of the Nativity of Mary

Knowing in advance
the course and outcome of all miseries
she soothes our fear
she awakens our faith
she strengthens our hope
she dispels our lack of confidence
she bolsters our timidness.

Are you afraid to approach the Father?
Terrified by the mere sound of his voice,
do you flee to the woods?

He has given you Jesus
as a mediator.

What can such a Son not gain
from such a Father?

He will be heard because of his humble submission.[1]
For the Father loves his Son.[2]

Or are you afraid of him, too?

He is your brother
and your own flesh,[3]
tempted in all things
yet without sin[4]
that he might be merciful. [5]

This is the brother
Mary gave to you.

But perhaps you fear the divine majesty in him
because although he became man
yet he remained God. [6]

Do you want to have an advocate with him?
Have recourse to Mary,

The humanity of Mary is pure
not only pure from all contamination
but also pure by the matchlessness of her nature.

With no shadow of doubt I say:
she will be heard for her humble submission.

The Son will listen to his Mother
and the Father to he Son.
Little children,
she is the ladder for sinners
she is my greatest ground of my confidence
she is the entire basis of my hope.

Why?

Can her Son drive her way
or support her when she is driven away?

Can the Son not hear
or not be heard?

Neither surely.

You have found grace with God
said the angel. [7]

And happily so!

She will always find grace
and her grace is all we need.

The wise virgin[8] asked,
not—like Solomon— for wisdom[9]
not for riches
not for power
but for grace.

And it by grace alone
that we are saved.

What else do we want, brothers?

Let us ask for grace
and let us ask through Mary
because she has found what she sought
and she cannot be disappointed. [10]

Let us ask for grace
but grace with God. [11]
For with human beings
grace is a delusion[12]

Let others ask for merit
let us eagerly seek grace.

Why?

Is it not by grace
that we are here?

Bernard *of* Clairvaux [13]

[1] *reverentia;* Heb 5:7
[2] Jn 5:20
[3] Cf Gen 37:27
[4] Heb 4:15
[5] Heb 2:17
[6] 1 Jn 2:1
[7] Lk 1:30

[8] Cf Mt 25:2
[9] 3 Kgs 3:11
[10] Mt 7:7
[11] Lk 1:30
[12] Cf Lk 2:52; Prov 1:30
[13] Sermon for the Feast of the Nativity of Mary, 6-8

Is it not true
that her children seem to recognize her
as their mother
by a kind of instinctive devotion
which faith gives them as second nature,
so that
first and foremost
in all their needs and dangers
they run to call upon her name
just as children run to their mother's breast?

I think it quite reasonable then
to understand of these children
that promise the prophet made to her:
Your children shall live in you[1] —
provided that the prophecy is always understood
to refer principally
to the Church.

Already
we really dwell
in the help of the mother of the Most High
We do live
in her protection,[2]
as if under the shadow of her wing.[3]

Afterwards
in participating in her glory
we shall be cherished
as if in her bosom.

Then a single cry of rejoicing and thanksgiving
will be heard
addressed to this mother:
'The dwelling place
of all of us
who rejoice and are glad[4]
is in you,
holy Mother of God.'

Guerric of Igny [5]

[1] Is 62:5
[2] Cf Ps 90:1,4
[3] Ps 16:8
[4] Ps 86:7
[5] Sermon 47.4: First Sermon for the Feast of the Assumption

God looked on the purity of his mother,
just as he had *looked on the humility of his handmaid.*[1]

Yes, God *looked on* her,
and while he looked,
he enriched her
and strengthened her
and rewarded her.

He looked indeed,
and saw that
—just as this most blessed of mothers
kept her virginity intact
despite the glory of her fruitfulness—
so her humility
remained intact and indestructible,
though she had reached the heights of perfection.

And it was in this way, as we said above,
that this most blessed womb
poured out its blessedness far and wide.

There was no question of careless waste,
but only of revealing the Sun of justice
to those who fear God.

In this way
his fervor glowed for him
above all others
and took its brightness from him:
greater brightness than anyone else received.

In short,
just as all grace and glory
flowed from this woman's body,
so it can be said
that every generation of saints truly arose from her
by what we can only call
the wonderful mystery of divine fruitfulness.

Let me repeat it:
the mother of Jesus
is not only the mother of our glorious head
Jesus Christ
mediator between God and man
but she is the mother
of all who love Jesus,
of the whole of Jesus sacred body.[2]

In fact, if Eve is said to be
the mother of all the living[3]
—though she brought us all forth to death
and became mother of wrath
for all who would one day arise from her—
how much more truly can we call Mary
the mother of the living?

To all generations of the faithful
she brought life
and she became for them
the mother of grace.

 John *of* Ford [4]

[1] Lk 1:48
[2] Cf 1 Co 6:15
[3] Cf Gn 3:20
[4] Sermon 70 on the Song of Songs, 5

Mary

—wishing to introduce the Beloved of her womb,
the Beloved of her desires,
into the affections of all her children—
describes him
not according to the flesh
but according to the spirit,
as if she too would say:
Even if I knew Christ according to the flesh,
now I know him so no longer.[1]

For she desires to form her Only-begotten
in all her children by adoption.

Although they have been brought to birth
by the word of truth,
nevertheless she brings them forth every day
by desire and devoted care
until they reach perfect manhood
according to the stature of the maturity of her Son[2]
whom she bore and brought forth
once and for all.

Indeed
as Isaiah said:
Before she was in labor
she brought forth[3]
because she brought forth without sorrow
nor did she experience the difficulty
and trouble of childbirth
when she brought forth the fruit of eternal gladness.

Commending this to us therefore
she says:
'I am the mother
of fair love
of fear
of knowledge
and of holy hope.'[4]

Is he then your son,
O virgin of virgins?

Is your beloved such a one as this,
O most beautiful of women?

'Clearly so,
my beloved is such a one
and he is my Son,
O daughters of Jerusalem.[5]
'My beloved is fair love in himself
He is fear,
hope,
and knowledge
in whoever is born of him.'[6]

For he is not only
the One we love
fear
and acknowledge
and in whom we hope,
but he it is
who brings about all those things
in us,
and as these virtues grow in strength
like the limbs and members of our body
they bring him to maturity and perfection
in us.

Then Christ will have been perfectly formed in you[7]
—as far as is possible in this life.

Then his own truth will have been made manifes
in you
if you have acknowledged the truth which is himself,
and, having acknowledged it,
you have glorified it
in fear as well as in hope.

And lest this hope should be in vain,
charity has also been poured into your heart.[8]

Guerric of Igny [9]

[1] 2 Cor 5:16
[2] Eph 4:13
[3] Is 66:7
[4] Sir 24:24 LXX
[5] Sg 5:9. 16
[6] Cf Jn 1:13
[7] Gal 4:19
[8] Rom 5:5
[9] Sermon 52.3: Second Sermon
for the Nativity of Mary

While [Gertrud] was praying ⅓
the Virgin Mother appeared to her
in the presence of the ever-to-be-venerated Trinity
in the likeness of a white lily with
—as is usual—
three petals:
one upright
two drooping.

By this
she was given to understand that
the blessed Mother of God herself
is thus worthily called
'the white lily of the Trinity'
because above every creature
she most fully and worthily received in herself
the virtues of the honored Trinity,
which not even the least speck of venial sin
had ever stained.

By the upright petal
was denoted the omnipotence of God the Father,
by the two drooping petals
the wisdom and goodness of the Son and Holy Spirit,
whom she is most like.

Then too she understood from the Blessed Virgin
that if anyone greeting her
devoutly called her
'White lily of the Trinity
and brightest rose of heavenly loveliness'
she would manifest in him most strikingly
what powers she holds
from the omnipotence of the Father,
what great knowledge she has
for the salvation of humankind
from the wisdom of the Son,
and how immeasurably fertile she is
in the bowels of loving-kindness
from the goodness of the Holy Spirit.

Gertrud *of* Helfta [1]

[1] The Herald of God's Loving-Kindness 3.19

She who is the only Virgin-Mother,
she who glories in having borne the Only-begotten of
the Father,
embraces that same Only-begotten of hers
in all his members
and so can be truly called mother of all
in whom she recognizes her Christ to have been
formed,
or in whom she knows he is being formed.

The first Eve
is not so much a mother as a stepmother
since she handed on to her children an inheritance
of certain death
rather than the beginning of light.
She is indeed called the mother of all the living[1]
but she turned out to be more precisely
the murderer of the living,
or mother of the dead,
since the only fruit of her child-bearing
was death.

And as Eve was incapable of fulfilling the vocation
of her title,
Mary consummated the mystery.

She herself
—like the Church of which she is the type—
is a mother
of all who are reborn to life.

She is in fact the mother of the Life
by which everyone lives
and when she brought it forth from herself
she in some way brought to rebirth
all those who were to live by that Life.

One was born,
but we were all reborn,
since in that seed which holds the power of rebirth
we were all already then in him.[2]

Just as from the beginning
we were in Adam
by the seed of carnal generation
so even before the beginning
we were there much more present in Christ
by the seed of spiritual regeneration.[3]

Thus
the blessed mother of Christ,
knowing that by reason of this mystery
she is the mother of all Christians
shows herself a mother by her care and loving
attention.

For her heart is not hardened against these children
as if they were not her own.
Her womb carried a child once only
yet it remains ever fruitful
never ceasing to bring forth
the fruits of her motherly compassion.

The blessed Fruit of your womb,[4]
O holy mother,
left you pregnant with inexhaustible tenderness.

He was born of you
once and for all,
yet he remains in you always,
making you forever fruitful.

Within the locked garden of your chastity
he makes the sealed well-spring[5] of charity
always abundant in its supply:
that the well-spring
though sealed
is yet channeled to the outer world
and its waters are at our disposal
in courtyard and street.

13

In short,
if the servant of Christ
by his care and heartfelt tenderness
bears his little children again and again
until Christ be formed in them,[6]
how much more is this true
of the very Mother of Christ?

Paul begot his children
by preaching the word of truth[7]
through which they were born again,
but Mary
in a manner far more holy and like to God,
by giving birth
to the Word himself.

Guerric of Igny,[8]

[1] Gen 3:20
[2] Heb 7:10
[3] 1 Cor 15:22
[4] Lk 1:42
[5] Sg 4:12
[6] Gal 4:19
[7] Jas 1:18
[8] Sermon 47.2-3: First Sermon
for the Feast of the Assumption

Milk is sweet
but if we churn it
it produces the richness of butter.

Heed carefully then
the depth of devotion with which
God wants us to honor her.

He has put the fulness of all good
in Mary
so that if we have any grounds
for hope
for grace
or for salvation
we know that it spills over
from her
who mounts up overflowing with delights. [1]

She is a garden of delights[2]
which, at its coming,
the divine southerly breeze
not only wafts over
but suffuses
until its scents waft and drift everywhere
giving off their aroma:
the gifts of graces.

Take away this sun-drenched body
which gives light to the world:
where is the day?

Take away Mary
this star of the sea
the sea truly great and wide:[3]
what is left but enveloping darkness
and the shadow of death
and the densest blackness?

With the very core our being then
with all the affections of our hearts
and with all our prayers
let us honor
Mary
because this is the will of Him
who wills that we posses all things
through Mary.

 Bernard *of* Clairvaux [4]

[1] Sg 8:5
[2] Sg 4:12-16
[3] Ps 103:25
[4] Sermon for the Feast of the Nativity of Mary, 6-7

How happy is she
who is both mother and spouse of God
the gate of heaven
the loveliness of paradise
lady of angels
queen of the universe
joy of the saints
advocate of believers
courage of those who fight
recaller of those who wander
medicine of the penitent.

O sure salvation!
Short path of life!
Sole hope of pardon
sweetness unique.

You, my Lady,
are my all.

In your hands
has been stored for me
the fulness of all good.

With you
have been hidden the unfailing treasures
of truth and grace
of peace and pity
of salvation and wisdom
of glory and honor.

You are my anchor amid the billows
my port in shipwreck
my support in tribulation
my comfort in grief.

For those who are yours
you are
aid in oppression
help in time of crisis
temperance in prosperity
joy in time of waiting
refreshment in toil.

Whatsoever I can stammer
in your praise
is less
than your praise
for you are worthy of all praise.

Adam *of* Perseigne [1]

She is loved
and praised
and honored by all.

For men and for angels,
she is
—after God—
the first [object of] love
and praise
and honor.

The whole church of the saints
proclaims her praises:
The daughters of Sion saw her
and declared her highly blessed;
the queens and concubines praised her. [1]

Nor does she herself pass over in silence this grace of
such great favor:
All generations, she says,
will call me blessed. [2]

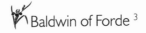Baldwin of Forde [3]

[1] Sg 6:8
[2] Lk 1:48
[3] Tractate 7

Some of our brothers
I believe can still be found alive today
who listened with me
to our blessed father and teacher[1]
praise the nobility of silence
—one of her greatest gifts—
in Mary
mother of God and greatest of all women.

In all the holy gospels
we find her words
a mere seven times.
Many times did she ponder in her heart
but seldom did she speak.

Certainly more than these few words
would have been written
had she said more,
especially because her frequent recollection
could have brought
only the most salutary and important words
from such a fullness of the Spirit.

We read that she spoke
twice to the angel
twice to Elizabeth
twice to her Son
and once to the servants at the wedding ♫

Perhaps it is not inappropriate
to draw a parallel
between the seven words of the most holy Virgin
and the equal number of gifts of the Holy Spirit.[2]

The spirit of the fear of the Lord
seems parallel to what she said to the servants:
Whatever he says to you,
keep and do.

As Wisdom teaches,
One who fears the Lord neglects nothing.[3]

That she intercedes mercifully
for what the suffering need
corresponds to the spirit of godliness.

That she asked
with an appropriately motherly voice:
Son, why have you treated us like this? ♫
can perhaps be attributed to the spirit of knowledge,
which deals rather with human
than with divine matters.

In the spirit of might and magnanimity
she indicated to Gabriel
—who was promising an inviolable conception—
her resolve to preserve her virginity:
How can this be, since I know not man? [4]

She answered him deliberately
in the spirit of counsel:
Behold the handmaid of the Lord.[5]

Her word of greeting
was filled with the spirit of understanding,
for on hearing it
the unborn forerunner
recognized the Lord's presence
and his mother
the joy of her exultant son.

[Elizabeth] understood
both Gabriel's announcement
and the mystery of the Lord's incarnation.

The virgin mother's response to her
was to exult in God
her Jesus, [6]
whose name had already been spoken by the angel. [7]

In the fullness of the spirit of wisdom
she burst forth in a song to his glory,
magnifying him
of whom she had heard that
he will be great,
who is truly one
with the Father
and the Holy Spirit
God,
over all and blessed forever.

Geoffrey of Auxerre [8]

[1] Bernard of Clairvaux, Occasional Sermons 52.1-3, and Sermon for Sunday within the octave of the Assumption, 10.
[2] Is 11:2-3 Vulg.
[3] Qo 7:19 Vulg.
[4] Lk 1:34.
[5] Lk 1:38.
[6] Cf Hab 3:18 Vulg.
[7] Lk 2:21.
[8] Sermon 14 on the Apocalypse.

Jesus said:

'At Vespers,
praise me in that most constant faith
by which the Blessed Virgin alone
at the time of my death
—when the apostles ran away
and all were despairing—
stood firm
unmoved in the truth faith.

She imitated me
in that faithfulness
by which,
already dead and taken down from the cross,
I pursued humankind
even to the limbo of hell
from which I snatched them
with the all-powerful hand of my mercy
and transported them to the joys of paradise.'

'At Compline
praise me in that most praiseworthy perseverance
by which my sweetest mother
persevered unto the end[1]
in all good deeds and virtues.

She imitated me
who carried out the task of human redemption
with such great care
that even after I had won true freedom
for humankind
by my most bitter death
nonetheless I did not fail to hand over
my incorruptible body
for burial in human fashion
to show that I would refuse nothing,
however vile
for human salvation.[1]

Gertrud *of* Helfta [2]

[1] Mt 10:22
[2] The Herald of God's Loving-Kindness 3.46

Come, my chosen one,
he says,
and I will set up my throne in you.[1]

There is no more expressive
or more fitting description
of her glorious privilege
than to say that
she is the throne of the God who reigns supreme.

The Divine Majesty
has never been seen to lavish his abundance
on any soul
so completely and so intimately
as on her
in whom before all others
he has especially chosen to reside.

≈

Come, my chosen one,
he says,
and I will set up my throne in you.

≈

You have sheltered the Child in your womb;
you will embrace the Infinite in the depths
of your soul.

You were the resting place for the Pilgrim;
you will be the palace of the Sovereign.

You were the tent of the Warrior
as he prepared for battle in the world;
you will be the throne of the Victor in heaven.

You were the bridal chamber of the Bridegroom in
the flesh,
you will be the throne of the King in all his majesty.

13

The virgin most prudent
had adorned her bridal chamber
both to receive you,
Christ
her King,
as guest,
and to hold you
as Bridegroom.

She adorned herself
I repeat,
with the manifold beauty and glory of virtue
and perhaps more lavishly because of her greater
poverty,
and it was all safer and surer
because more interior.

That beauty invited you to come;
it allured you to return.

By entering
you increased the grace of blessing,
by returning
you multiplied it beyond all measure.

When you entered you were born as man in her;
when you returned you were glorified as God in her.

Then you made in her
a shrine of grace for yourself;
now you have set her up as a throne of glory.

Guerric of Igny [2]

[1] Responsory sung at Vigils in honor of a virgin
[2] Sermon 47.5-6: First Sermon on the Feast of the Assumption

For behold, from this day
all generations shall call me blessed.[1] ♫

'Behold', she says.
—This is an injunction used by someone
who both perceives and shows.

Behold,
I now see
what is going to be done through me
what fruit is going to derive from me
how many enormous benefits
are going to come through me
not for myself alone
but for all ♫

All generations will be blessed through my fruit
and since they all will be blessed
they all will call me singularly blessed:
all generations
the generations of heaven
and the generations of earth
all the angels
and all the elect.
♫

The number of generations among the angels

will be restored through the One
begotten through me,
and the human race
which had been condemned in Adam
will be reborn to eternal bliss
through the blessed fruit of my womb.

Within these
and indeed beyond all
these generations
all generations shall call me blessed!

Deservedly, therefore,
O Queen,
will all generations call you blessed.

You have given birth
to true eternal bliss
for all generations.

Bernard of Clairvaux [2]

[1] Lk 1:48
[2] Sentences, series 3.127

Blessed Virgin,
if there be anyone
who remembers having called upon
your mercy in need
and it was lacking,
let him be silent.

For we your humble servants
delight with you in your other virtues,
but this one we claim
for ourselves.

We praise your virginity,
we marvel at your humility;
but your mercy tastes sweet to the merciful
and we embrace your mercy
with greater affection
reflect on it more often
and invoke it more frequently.

For it is this
which gained a cure for the whole world
and obtained salvation for every person.

For everyone know
that you represented the entire human race
when you were told
Do not be afraid, Mary,
for you have found grace[1]
as you asked.

Who then can explore
the length and breadth
the height and depth[2]
of your mercy,
o blessed one?

Its length reaches even to the day of judgement
to all those who call upon it.

Its breadth fills the whole earth
so that the whole earth is filled with your mercy.

Its height attains the restoration of the eternal city
and its depth gains redemption
for those who sit
in darkness and the shadow of death.[3]

Through you
heaven is filled
hell is emptied
the ruins of the heavenly Jerusalem are rebuilt
and lost life is given to those who wait
in wretchedness.

The utterly powerful and sympathetic charity
both in its compassionate attachment
and its supportive achievement
is equally rich in both.

To this fount therefore
may our thirsting souls hasten.
To this mound of mercy
may our distress race with reverence.

Bernard *of* Clairvaux [4]

[1] Lk 1:30
[2] Cf. Eph 3:18
[3] Lk 1:79
[4] Sermon Four for the Feast of the Assumption, 8-9

Mary
has been exalted
above the choirs of angels.

The Mother
can contemplate
nothing above herself
but her Son alone.

The Queen
can gaze in wonder
at nothing above herself
but the King.

The Mediatrix
can venerate
nothing above herself
but the Mediator.

May she
by her prayers
represent
reconcile
and commend us
to her Only begotten Son
Jesus Christ
to whom be honor and glory
for endless ages.

Guerric of Igny [1]

[1] Sermon 47.6: First Sermon for the Feast of the Assumption

And the virgin's name was Mary.[1]

Let us say a few words about this name
which means
'star of the sea'
and is so appropriate to
the Virgin Mother.

Surely she is very appropriately likened to a star.

The star sends forth its ray
without harm to itself.

In the same way
the Virgin brought forth her son
with no injury to herself.

The ray no more diminishes the star's brightness
than does the Son his mother's integrity.

She is indeed
that noble star
risen out of Jacob[2]
whose beam enlightens this earthly globe.

She it is
whose brightness
both twinkles in the highest heaven
and pierces the pit of hell[3]
and is shed upon earth
warming our hearts far more than our bodies,
fostering virtue
and cauterizing vice.

She
—I tell you—
is that splendid and wondrous star
suspended as by necessity
over this great wide sea
radiant with merit and brilliant in example.

O you
whoever you are
who feel that in the tidal wave of this world
you are nearer to being tossed about
among the squalls and gales
than treading on dry land:
if you do not want to founder in the tempest
do not avert your eyes from the brightness of this star.

When the wind of temptation blows up within you
when you strike upon the rock of tribulation
gaze up at this star
call out to Mary

Whether you are being tossed about by the waves
of pride or ambition
or slander or jealousy
gaze up at this star
call out to Mary.

When rage or greed or fleshly desires are battering
the skiff of your soul
gaze up at Mary.

When the immensity of your sins weighs you down
and you are bewildered by the loathsomeness
of your conscience
when the terrifying thought of judgement appalls you
and you begin to founder
in the gulf of sadness an despair
think of Mary.

In dangers
in hardships[4]
in every doubt
think of Mary
call out to Mary.

Keep her in your mouth
keep her in your heart.

Follow the example of her life
and you will obtain the favor
of her prayer.

Following her
you will never go astray.

Asking her help
you will never despair.

Keeping her in your thoughts
you will never wander away.

With your hand in hers
you will never stumble.

With her protecting you
you will not be afraid.

With her leading you
you will never tire.

Her kindness
will see you through to the end.

Then you will know
by your own experience
how true it is that
the Virgin's name was Mary.

Bernard *of* Clairvaux [5]

[1] Lk 1:27
[2] Num 24:17
[3] Cf Prov 5:5
[4] 2 Cor 6:4
[5] Homily Two in Praise of the Blessed Virgin Mary, 17

All our confidence
lies in the childbearing
of our Virgin
and though I may be unworthy
I shall not cease to dwell upon her praises.

If you stand in need of mercy
it is found in full measure
in the heart of the Virgin.

If you reverence the truth
give thanks to the Virgin
since from the ground
of her virgin flesh
has arisen the truth
which you worship.

No less give thanks
to the Virgin
if you follow after peace
since from her
is born for you
the peace which passes all understanding.[1]

If you pursue justice
see that you are not ungrateful
to the Virgin
for at the opening of her womb
justice looked down from heaven. [2]

if your faith is shaken by assault from an enemy
turn your eyes
to the Virgin
and what was wavering
will be firmly fixed.

If the lust of the flesh delights you
turn your gaze
to the Virgin
and the danger to your chastity
will be removed.

If pride disturbs your spirit
turn your gaze
to the Virgin
and by the merit of her unsullied humility
your swelling spirit will subside.

If you are set on fire by anger's torches
lift your eyes
to the Virgin
and you will grow gentle
through her calm.

If ignorance or error have led you astray
from the way of life
look to Mary, star of the sea,
and in her light
you will be led back to the path of truth.

If the vice of avarice
commands your idolatrous worship
call to mind
the generosity of the Virgin
and with a love of poverty
there will come to you
the goodness of openhandedness.

In every peril
the goodness of the Virgin comes to succour
and power to succour it is.

Give thanks
for her childbearing;
from her fulness
the sum total of graces has flowed.

For us
the Virgin brought forth.
Ours is the birth.
For us
the Child was born
and to us
the Son was given. [3]

Adam *of* Perseigne [4]

[1] Cf Ph 4:7
[2] Cf Ps 85:11, 1 Co 1:30
[3] Is 9:6
[4] Letter 3.28

The sole and whole Christ
—Head and Body—
is one.

And this one
—both many children and One Child—
comes of
one God in heaven
and
one mother on earth.

As head and members
are one Child
and many children
so Mary and the Church
are one Mother
and more than one Mother.

Each is mother
and each is virgin.

Each without lust conceives
by the same Spirit;
each without sin produces offspring
for God the Father.

Without any sin whatever
Mary brought forth
the Head of the body;
the Church
through the very forgiveness of all sin[1]
has given birth to the
body of the Head.

Each is Mother of Christ
yet neither
gives birth
to the Whole Christ
without the other.

The result is
that in the divinely inspired Scriptures
what is true of
Virgin-Mother Church
in general
is true of
Virgin-Mother Mary
in particular.
And what applies properly
And whether either one or the other
is in question
there is practically no need
to differentiate between them.

Every true believer can be described
in her own way
as bride of the divine Word
the mother
and daughter
and sister
of Christ
and so
both virgin and mother.

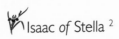Isaac *of Stella* [2]

[1] Cf. Ac 2:38
[2] Sermon 51.7: First Sermon for the Feast of the Assumption

Whatever [Gertrud] heard read or chanted
in praise or salutation
of the Blessed Virgin
or of other saints,
which could gently sway her love,
through it
she always concentrated more
—as was utterly right—
on the King of kings,
the Lord who is above all,
the one and only Beloved and Chosen One,
than on the very saints
whose feast or commemoration
was being celebrated.

And so
on the feast of the Lord's Annunciation
—when the Blessed Virgin was repeatedly praised
in the sermon
and no mention was made of the saving work
of the Lord's Incarnation—
she found this irksome.

And returning from the sermon,
as she was walking past the altar
of the glorious Virgin,
in greeting her
she sensed that she was not completely moved
by gentle love
towards that mother of all grace.

Rather, in every salutation and praise of hers,
she was always concentrating more lovingly on Jesus,
the blessed fruit of her womb.

Because of this
she began to fear
that she was incurring the wrath
of so powerful a queen.

The kindly Comforter softly set her fear aside,
saying
'Do not be afraid, dearest,
that your greeting or praise of my dear mother
is such that you concentrate more on me.
She greatly delights in this.

'Since your conscience troubles you for this,
another time be eager to greet the image
of my chaste mother
before the altar with more devotion,
leaving my image ungreeted.'

'Far be it from me, Lord,
my only or rather complete Good!'
she replied.
'For my heart can never consent to this
that I should abandon you
on whom depends all the salvation
or rather the very life of my soul
and that I direct my affection to greet someone else.'

Gently the Lord replied:
'Give me your consent now, my love.
and as often as you greet my mother in this way
and pass me over,
I shall accept it
and reward it
as that perfection with which some truly faithful
person readily leaves me,
the hundredfold of all hundredfolds,
for my greater glory.'

Gertrud the Great [1]

[1] The Herald of God's Loving-Kindness 3.20

What exhibits more plainly
the power and merit of faith
than that the virgin conceived God by faith,
and by faith deserved to have all
that God had promised her
fulfilled?

Blessed is she who believed,
we read,
for what was told her by the Lord
shall be brought to fulfillment.[1]

She who conceived God
by faith
promises you the same
if you have faith.

If you will faithfully receive the word
from the mouth of the heavenly messenger
you too may conceive the God
whom the whole world cannot contain,
conceive him in your heart
not in your body.

Guerric of Igny [2]

[1] Lk 1:45
[2] Sermon 48.4: Second Sermon for the Feast of the Annunciation

The Virgin is that royal road
by which the Saviour approaches
proceeding from her womb
like a bridegroom from his chamber.

13

O blessed discoverer of grace,
bearer of life
mother of salvation:
through you
may we have access to your Son,
that he who was given to us
through you
may through you receive us.

May your integrity
exonerate the guilt of our corruption,
and may the humility pleasing to God
solicit forgiveness for our vainglory.

May your lavish love
cloak the multitude of our sins
and may your glorious fruitfulness
confer on us the fruitfulness of deserving.

Our Lady
our Mediatrix
our Advocate,
reconcile us to your Son
commend us to your Son
and represent us before him.

O blessed Lady,
through the grace
which you have found,
through the favor
which you deserved
through the mercy
to which you gave birth,
bring it about that
Christ Jesus, your Son, our Lord.
who by your mediation
deigned to share our weakness and wretchedness
may by your intercession
make us sharers of his glory and blessedness.

Bernard *of* Clairvaux [1]

[1] Second Sermon for Advent, 5

Whatever we say in praise of the mother
touches the Son:
of this there is no doubt.

And when we honor the Son
we detract nothing
from the mother's glory.

For if, as Solomon says:
A wise son is the glory of his father.[1]
How much more glorious is it
to become the mother of Wisdom himself?

But how can I attempt to praise her
whom the prophets have proclaimed
the angel has acknowledged
and the Evangelist has described
as praiseworthy?

I will not praise her then.
I dare not do so.
I will only mull over devoutly
what the Holy Spirit has already said
by the mouth of the Evangelist.

Bernard *of* Clairvaux[2]

[1] Pr 13:1
[2] Homily Four in Praise of the Blessed Virgin Mary, 1

O Mother of Mercy,
be replete
in the glory of your Son
and leave your scraps
to your little ones.

You are now
at table,
Lady;
under the table
we puppies are waiting.[1]

As the eyes of a handmaid
look to the hands of her mistress[2]
so this famished family
is looking to you
for the food of life.

Through you
we have partaken of the fruit of life
at the table of the existing sacraments;
through you
at the table of joy everlasting
may we partake of the very fruit of life:
Jesus
the fruit of your womb
to whom be honor and glory
for ever and ever.

Guerric of Igny[3]

[1] Cf. Mt 15:27
[2] Ps 123:2
[3] Sermon 50.9: Fourth Sermon for the Feast of the Assumption

The Authors

Adam of Perseigne

A man of humble origins, Adam was ordained a priest and served as chaplain at the court of the Countess of Champagne before becoming, in succession, a Canon Regular, a Benedictine, and finally a Cistercian monk, probably at Pontigny. Sometime in the 1180s he became abbot of Perseigne in Normandy, the continental home of the kings of England, and adviser to Richard the Lionhearted. He died about 1221.

Aelred of Rievaulx

The son of a line of hereditary priests at Hexham, in Northumberland, northern England, Aelred was raised at the court of King David of Scotland. After a chance visit in 1134, he entered the new abbey of Rievaulx in Yorkshire and was soon made novice master, charged with training new recruits. He served as abbot of Revesby, a daughter-house of Rievaulx, before returning home to become abbot. Protesting his lack of ability, he began writing at the insistence of Saint Bernard, and is sometimes known as 'the Bernard of the north'. After a long and debilitating struggle with arthritis, he died in 1167.

Amadeus
of Lausanne

As a child, Amadeus was taken to a cistercian abbey by his father, intent on leaving the world. After about three years, however, his father removed himself and his son to the great benedictine abbey of Cluny, and then sent his son on to Germany for an education. By 1125, the young Amadeus was at the door of Clairvaux, asking to be admitted as a Cistercian. He later became bishop of Lausanne.

Baldwin of Forde

Before becoming a Cistercian monk in 1169, Baldwin was the archdeacon of Exeter, in southwestern England. Within six years he had been elected abbot, the first of a series of responsibilities which led him to the bishopric of Worcester and archbishopric of Canterbury. Homilies he preached at Forde (or Ford) Abbey he later reworked for publication as treatises. Having preached a crusade throughout Wales in 1188, Baldwin took the cross and died during a siege at Acre.

Bernard of Clairvaux

'The Mellifluous Doctor' of the Church, whose magnificent rhetorical style and intense dedication to Christ made him the counsellor of popes and kings during the first half of the twelfth century. Born to minor nobility in 1090, he persuaded thirty of his relatives and friends to enter monastic life with him when he entered Citeaux at the age of about twenty-two, and within two years he was named abbot of a new foundation at Clairvaux. During the last years of his life, he was often absent from his beloved monastery, travelling Europe on behalf of the pope and founding cistercian abbeys in his wake. Yet he managed to leave an impressive literary inheritance which has been read continuously since his death on 20 August 1153.

Geoffrey of Auxerre A student of Peter Abelard at Paris, Geoffrey abandoned whatever career he had embarked on after hearing Bernard of Clairvaux preach on conversion. He became Bernard's secretary and close companion, collecting information and contributing to the Life of Bernard written with a view to his canonization. In later years he served as abbot of four monasteries—Igny, Clairvaux, Fossanova, and Hautecombe, before retiring to Clairvaux in 1188.

Gilbert of Hoyland Abbot of Swineshead in the fens of Lincolnshire, Gilbert may have been a monk of Clairvaux who was sent to northern England to help the monks of 'hollandia' make the transition to cistercian life when the White Monks absorbed the Savignac Order and its monasteries of monks and of nuns in 1147. That some of his sermons were clearly preached to nuns supports this supposition. A great admirer of Bernard and a friend of Aelred of Rievaulx, Gilbert died in 1172.

Guerric of Igny Born and educated at the noted cathedral school at Tournai, in modern Belgium, Guerric visited the abbey of

Clairvaux as a seasoned scholar, with no intention of staying. Urged by the always persuasive Bernard to abandon academic life for the cloister, Guerric became a monk, and later abbot of Igny, near the royal French city of Reims. He died in 1157.

Isaac of Stella

Arriving in France from his native England early in the 1120s, Isaac was familiar, and not unsympathetic, with the work of Peter Abelard and Gilbert of Poitiers–both leading academics of the day and both criticized by Saint Bernard. Elected abbot of Stella (L'Etoile) in 1147, Isaac vigorously defend the exiled Thomas Becket of Canterbury and as a result ended his own life in exile on the Isle of Ré, off the western coast of France, sometime around 1169.

John of Ford

As abbot of Ford, the same Ford(e) where Baldwin had served, John had to contend with an interdict imposed against King John the Landless and with the crippling taxation the king levied to support a military campaign in Ireland. Taking up the task of finishing a sermon-commentary on the Song of Songs begun by Saint Bernard and continued by Gilbert of Hoyland, John completed the task in one hundred twenty sermons before dying in 1214.

Stephen of Sawley

Stephen entered monastic life at Fountains Abbey–today an imposing monastic ruin and educational centre in northern England–and before his death in 1252, he served successively as abbot of Sawley (Salley) in south Yorkshire and of Newminster in Northumbria–both today marked by only fragmentary remains. While he drew heavily on the works of Bernard, William, Aelred and Gilbert of Hoyland, his written works reflect a combination of cistercian austerity and the gentler piety of the mid thirteenth century.

William of Saint Thierry

A scholar and a benedictine abbot, William recognized in Saint Bernard at their first meeting the contemplative monastic life he longed for. Although he waited for some fifteen years before entering the newly founded cistercian abbey of Signy in the Ardenne forest of northeastern France, his works as a Benedictine already reflect his conversion to the Cistercians. It was William who first called Bernard's attention to what they considered the errors of Peter Abelard, and William who composed the first book of the Life of Bernard, whom he preceded in death in 1148.

The Sources

The translations have sometimes been altered or abridged slightly to fit the format.

Adam of Perseigne
> *The Letters of Adam of Perseigne, 1*
> Translated by Grace Perigo

Aelred of Rievaulx
> *Liturgical Sermons, 1. The First Clairvaux Collection.*
> Translated by Theodore Berkeley OCSO and M. Basil Pennington OCSO.

> *Treatises 1.* On Jesus at the Age of Twelve; Rule for A Recluse; The Pastoral Prayer.
> Translated by Theodore Berkeley OCSO, Mary Paul Macpherson OCSO, Penelope Lawson CSMV.

Amadeus of Lausanne
> *Eight Homilies on the Praises of Blessed Mary.*
> Translated by Grace Perigo

Baldwin of Forde
> *The Commendation of Faith.*
> Translated by Jane Patricia Freeman and David N. Bell

> *Spiritual Tractates,* 2 volumes.
> Translated by David N. Bell

Bernard of Clairvaux
> *The Letters*
> Translated by Bruno Scott James

Parables and Sentences
Translated by Michael Casey OCSO and Francis R. Swietek

Homilies in Praise of the Blessed Virgin Mary
Translated by Marie-Bernard Saïd OSB

Sermons on the Song of Songs, 4 volumes
Translated by Kilian Walsh OCSO and Irene Edmonds

Sermons for Advent and the Christmas Season
Translated by Irene Edmonds, Wendy Mary Beckett, and Conrad
Greenia OCSO

Autumn Sermons
Translated by Irene Edmonds

Occasional Sermons
Translated by Conrad Greenia OCSO and Hugh McCaffery OCSO

Geoffrey of Auxerre
On the Apocalypse
Translated by Joseph Gibbons

Gertrud the Great of Helfta
The Herald of God's Loving-Kindness, 2 volumes
Translated by Alexandra Barratt

Gilbert of Hoyland
Sermons on the Song of Songs, 3 volumes
Translated by Lawrence C. Braceland SJ

Guerric of Igny
Liturgical Sermons, 2 volumes
Translated by monks of Mount Saint Bernard Abbey

Isaac of Stella
Sermons on the Christian Year, 2 volumes
Translated by Hugh McCaffery OCSO

John of Ford
> *Sermons on the Final Verses of the Song of Songs,* 7 volumes
> Translated by Wendy Mary Beckett

Stephen of Sawley
> *Treatises:* Meditations on the Joys of the Virgin Mary;
> The Threefold Exercise; A Mirror for Novices; On
> the Recitation of the Divine Office
> Translated by Jeremiah F. O'Sullivan; edited by Bede
> K. Lackner O.Cist.

William of Saint Thierry
> *The Mirror of Faith*
> Translated by Thomas X. Davis OCSO

Typography
by Gale Akins at
Humble Hills Press
Kalamazoo, Michigan

Text type is *ITC Golden Cockerel*
1996 revival by Dave Farey & Richard Dawson
of the 1929 original
by Eric Gill for the
Golden Cockerel Press, England.
Source names *set in Eric Gill's*
Gill Sans light, 1928-30.
Ornaments designed by Eric Gill.
Heads *and* First Text Lines
Codex, by Georg Trump, 1954-56.